How to File for Divorce in North Carolina

with forms

Jacqueline D. Stanley
Edward A. Haman
Attorneys at Law

Sphinx® Publishing
A Division of Sourcebooks, Inc.®
Naperville, IL • Clearwater, FL

Published by: **Sphinx® Publishing, A Division of Sourcebooks, Inc.®**

Naperville Office
P.O. Box 4410
Naperville, Illinois 60567-4410
630-961-3900
Fax: 630-961-2168

Clearwater Office
P.O. Box 25
Clearwater, Florida 34617
727-587-0999
Fax: 727-586-5088

Interior Design and Production: Shannon E. Harrington, Sourcebooks, Inc.®

Library of Congress Cataloging-in-Publication Data

Stanley, Jacqueline D.
How to file for divorce in North Carolina : with forms /
Jacqueline D. Stanley, Edward A. Haman.—2nd ed.
p. cm.
ISBN 1-57071-326-X (pbk.)
1. Divorce—Law and legislation—North Carolina—Popular works.
2. Divorce—Law and legislation—North Carolina—Forms. I. Haman,
Edward A. II. Title.
KFN7500.Z9S73 1998
346.75601'66—dc21 97-41509
CIP

Printed and bound in the United States of America.

HS Paperback – 10 9 8 7 6 5 4 3

Contents

Using Self-Help Law Books

Whenever you shop for a product or service, you are faced with various levels of quality and price. In deciding upon which product or service to buy, you make a cost/value analysis based upon what you are willing to pay and the quality you desire.

When buying a car you decide whether you want transportation, comfort, status, or sex appeal. Accordingly, you decide among such choices as a Neon, a Lincoln, a Rolls Royce, or a Porsche. Before making a decision, you usually weigh the merits of each option against the cost.

When you get a headache, you can take a pain reliever (such as aspirin) or visit a medical specialist for a neurological examination. Given this choice, most people, of course, take a pain reliever, since it costs only pennies, whereas a medical examination costs hundreds of dollars and takes a lot of time. This is usually a logical choice because rarely is anything more than a pain reliever needed for a headache. But in some cases, a headache may indicate a brain tumor, and failing to see a specialist right away can result in complications. Should everyone with a headache go to a specialist? Of course not, but people treating their own illnesses must realize that they are betting, on the basis of their cost/value analysis of the situation, that they are taking the most logical option.

The same cost/value analysis must be made in deciding to do one's own legal work. Many legal situations are very straightforward, requiring a simple form and no complicated analysis. Anyone with a little intelligence and a book of instructions can handle the matter simply.

But there is always the chance that complications are involved that only an attorney would notice. To simplify the law into a book like this, several legal cases often must be condensed into a single sentence or paragraph. Otherwise, the book would be several hundred pages long and too complicated for most people. However, this simplification necessarily leaves out many details and nuances which would apply to special or unusual situations. Also, there are many ways to interpret most legal questions. Your case may come before a judge who disagrees with the analysis of our authors.

Therefore, in deciding to use a self-help law book and to do your own legal work, you must realize that you are making a cost/value analysis, and are deciding that the chance your case will not turn out to your satisfaction is outweighed by the money you will save by doing it yourself. Most people handling their own simple legal matters never have a problem, but occasionally people find that it ended up costing them more to have an attorney straighten out the situation than it would have if they had hired an attorney in the beginning. Keep this in mind while handling your case, and be sure to consult an attorney if you feel you might need further guidance.

INTRODUCTION

Going through a divorce is probably one of the most common, and most traumatic, encounters with the legal system. Paying a divorce lawyer can be one of the most expensive bills to pay, and at a time when you are least likely to have extra funds. In a contested divorce case it is not uncommon for the parties to run up legal bills of over $10,000; and horror stories abound of lawyers charging substantial fees with little progress to show for it. This book is designed to enable you to obtain a divorce without hiring a lawyer. Even if you do hire a lawyer, this book will help you to work with him or her more effectively, which can also reduce your legal fees.

This is not a law school course, but a practical guide to get you through "the system" as easily as possible. Legal jargon has been nearly eliminated. For ease of understanding, this book uses the term *spouse* to refer to your husband or wife (whichever applies), and the terms *child* and *children* are used interchangeably.

Please keep in mind that different judges, and courts in different counties, may have their own particular (if not peculiar) procedures and ways of doing things. The court clerk's office can often tell you if they have any special forms or requirements. Court clerks cannot give legal advice, but they can tell you what their court or judges require.

The first two chapters of this book will give you an overview of the law and the legal system. Chapters 3, 4, and 5 will help you decide if you want an attorney and if you want a divorce. The remaining chapters will show you what forms you need, how to fill out the forms, and what procedures to follow. You will also find two appendices in the back of this book. Appendix A contains selected portions of the North Carolina law dealing with property division, alimony, and child support. Although these provisions are discussed in the book, it is sometimes helpful to read the law exactly as the legislature wrote it.

Finally, appendix B contains the forms you will use. You will not need to use all of the forms. This book will tell you which forms you need, depending upon your situation.

Before using any of the forms, be sure to read AN INTRODUCTION TO LEGAL FORMS, in chapter 6.

1 Marriage "Ins and Outs"

Several years (or maybe only months) ago you made a decision to get married. This chapter will discuss, in a general way, what you got yourself into, and how you can get yourself out.

Marriage

Marriage is frequently referred to as a contract. It is a legal contract, and, for many, it is also a religious contract. This book will deal only with the legal aspects. The wedding ceremony involves the bride and groom reciting certain vows, which are actually mutual promises about how they will treat each other. There are also legal papers signed, such as a marriage license and a marriage certificate. These formalities create certain rights and obligations for the husband and wife. Although the focus at the ceremony is on the emotional and romantic aspects of the relationship, the legal reality is that financial and property rights are being created. It is these financial and property rights and obligations that cannot be broken without a legal proceeding.

Marriage will give each of the parties certain rights in property, and it creates certain obligations with respect to the support of any children they have together (or adopt). Unfortunately, most people don't fully realize that these rights and obligations are being created until it comes time for a divorce.

Divorce

A divorce is the most common method of terminating or breaking the marriage contract. In a divorce, the court declares the marriage contract broken; divides the parties' property and debts; decides if either party should receive alimony; and determines the custody, support, and visitation with respect to any children the parties may have. Traditionally, a divorce could only be granted under certain specific circumstances, such as for *adultery*, or *mental cruelty*. Today, either party may petition the court for a divorce after they have lived *separate and apart* from their spouse for one year. Separate and apart means that one spouse lives in one place and the other spouse lives in another.

No Fault Divorce

North Carolina is a *no fault* divorce state. There is nothing for your spouse to contest other than the fact that you have been separated. This rarely happens because it is so easy to prove you have lived in one place and they in another. It is important to note that isolated incidents of sexual intercourse during the separation will not require your time to begin again. However, if you and your spouse reconcile and move back in together it will alter your date of separation.

Insanity

Another ground for divorce is the incurable insanity of a spouse. Obtaining a divorce on this ground often involves complex court procedures. If you are seeking a divorce because your spouse is incurably insane, you should consult a lawyer.

Annulment

The basic difference between a divorce and an annulment is that a divorce says, "this marriage is broken," and an annulment says, "there never was a marriage." An annulment is more difficult and often more complicated to prove, so it is not used very often. Annulments are only possible in a few circumstances, usually where one party deceived the other. If you decide that you want an annulment, you should consult an attorney. If you are seeking an annulment for religious reasons and need to go through a church procedure (rather than, or in addition to, a legal procedure), you should consult your priest or minister.

A divorce is generally easier to get than an annulment. This is because all you need to prove to get a divorce is that you have been separated for one year. How do you prove this? Simply by saying it. The DIVORCE COMPLAINT (Form 9 or Form 14), reads: "The Plaintiff and Defendant have lived continuously separate and apart from each other for more than one year immediately preceding the filing of this petition." That is all you need to do. However, in order to get an annulment you'll need to prove more. This proof will involve introducing various documents into evidence, and having other people come to testify at the court hearing.

GROUNDS FOR ANNULMENT

Annulments can only be granted under one of the following circumstances:

1. One of the parties was too young to get married. In North Carolina, both parties must be at least eighteen years old to get married. (There are a few exceptions, such as where the woman is pregnant and at least twelve years old or the underage person has parental consent.)
2. If one of the parties is physically impotent.
3. If one party didn't have the mental capacity to get married. This means the person was suffering from mental illness or mental disability (such as being severely retarded), to such an extent that the person didn't understand he or she was getting married; or didn't even understand the concept of marriage.

4. If one party was already married to another person. This might occur if one party married, mistakenly believing his divorce from his previous spouse was final.

5. If the marriage is incestuous. North Carolina prohibits marriage between certain family members, such as brother and sister, aunt and nephew, or uncle and niece.

If your spouse wants to stop an annulment, there are several arguments he or she could make to further complicate the case. This area of the law is not as well defined as divorce. There are no North Carolina Statutes outlining the proper procedures to follow, and annulments are much less common than divorces. The annulment procedure can be extremely complicated, and should not be attempted without consulting a lawyer.

Legal Separation

North Carolina law provides a means for parties to obtain a *legal separation*. This procedure is referred to in North Carolina as a *divorce from bed and board*. This procedure is used to divide property and provide for child support in cases where the husband and wife live separately, but remain married. It is sometimes used to break the financial rights and obligations of a couple whose religion does not permit divorce.

Grounds for Legal Separation

As a general rule, courts will only grant a divorce from bed and board in cases where one party is guilty of one or more of the following:

1. abandonment;

2. cruel and barbarous treatment that endangers the life of their spouse;

3. committing indignities to the person of the other that render their condition intolerable and life burdensome;

4. excessive use of alcohol or drugs;

5. adultery; or
6. maliciously turning their spouse out of doors.

The procedure for obtaining a divorce from bed and board is beyond the scope of this book. If you think you might be eligible for a divorce from bed and board, you should consult an attorney.

2 The Legal System

This chapter will give you a general introduction to the legal system. There are things you need to know in order to obtain a divorce (or help your lawyer get the job done), and to get through any encounter with the legal system with a minimum of stress. These are some of the realities of our system. If you don't learn to accept these realities, you will experience much stress and frustration.

Theory vs. Reality

Our legal system is a system of rules. There are basically three types of rules:

1. Rules of Law: These are the basic substance of the law, such as a law telling a judge how to go about dividing your property.
2. Rules of Procedure: These outline how matters are to be handled in the courts, such as requiring court papers to be in a certain form, or filed within a certain time.
3. Rules of Evidence: These set forth the manner in which facts are to be proven.

The theory is that these rules allow each side to present evidence most favorable to that side, and an independent person or persons (the judge or jury) will be able to figure out the truth. Then certain legal principles will be applied to that "truth" which will give a fair resolution of the dispute between the parties. These legal principles are supposed to be relatively unchanging so that we can all know what will happen in any given situation and can plan our lives accordingly. This will provide order and predictability to our society. Any change in the legal principles is supposed to occur slowly, so that the expected behavior in our society is not confused from day-to-day. Unfortunately, the system does not really work this way. What follows are only some of the problems in the real legal system:

The system is not perfect. Contrary to how it may seem, legal rules are not made just to complicate things and confuse everyone. They are attempts to make the system fair and just. They have been developed over several hundred years, and in most cases they do make sense. Unfortunately, our efforts to find fairness and justice have resulted in a complex set of rules. The legal system affects our lives in important ways, and it is not a game. However, it can be compared to a game in some ways. The rules are designed to apply to all people, in all cases. Sometimes the rules don't seem to give a fair result in a certain situation, but the rules are still followed. Just as a referee can make a bad call, so can a judge. There are also cases where one side wins by cheating.

Judges don't always follow the rules. This is a shocking discovery for many young lawyers. After spending three years in law school learning legal theory, and after spending countless hours preparing for a hearing and having all of the law on your side, you find that the judge isn't going to pay any attention to legal theories and the law. Many judges are going to make a decision simply on what they think seems fair under the circumstances. This concept is actually being taught in some law schools now. Unfortunately, what "seems fair" to a particular judge may depend upon his personal ideas and philosophy. For example, there is nothing in the divorce laws that gives one parent priority in child custody; however, a vast majority of judges believe that a child is generally better off with its mother. All other things being equal, these judges will find a way to justify awarding custody to the mother.

The system is often slow. Even lawyers get frustrated at how long it can take to get a case completed (especially if they don't get paid until it's done). Whatever your situation, things will take longer than you expect. Patience is required to get through the system with a minimum of stress. Don't let your impatience or frustration show. No matter what happens, keep calm, and be courteous.

No two cases are alike. Just because your friend's case went a certain way doesn't mean yours will have the same result. The judge can make a difference, and more often the circumstances will make a difference. Just because your co-worker makes the same income as you and has the same number of children, you can't assume you will be ordered to pay the same amount of child support. There are usually other circumstances your co-worker doesn't tell you about, and possibly doesn't understand.

Half of the people "lose." Remember, there are two sides to every legal issue, and there is usually only one winner. Especially if you let the judge decide, don't expect to have every detail go your way.

Divorce Law and Procedure

This section will give you a general overview of the law and procedures involved in getting a divorce. To most people, including lawyers, the law appears very complicated and confusing. Fortunately, many areas of the law can be broken down into simple and logical steps. Divorce is one of those areas. Law and the legal system are often compared to games, and just like games, it is important to know the players:

THE PLAYERS

The judge. The judge has the power to decide whether you can get divorced, how your property will be divided, which of you will get custody of the children, and how much the other will pay for child support. The judge is the last person you want to make angry with you! In general, judges have large caseloads and like it best when your case can be concluded quickly and without hassle. This means that the more you and your spouse agree upon, and the more complete your paperwork is, the better the judge will like it. Most likely, your only direct contact with the judge will be at the final hearing, which may last as little as five minutes. (See chapter 6 for more about how to deal with the judge.)

The judge's secretary. The judge's secretary sets the hearings for the judge, and can frequently answer many of your questions about the procedure and what the judge would like or require. Once again, you don't want to make an enemy of the secretary. This means that you don't call him or her often, and don't ask too many questions. A few questions are okay, and you may want to start off saying that you just want to make sure you have everything in order for the judge. You'll get much farther by being nice than by arguing.

The court clerk. Where the secretary usually only works for one judge, the court clerk handles the files for all of the judges. The clerk's office is the central place where all of the court files are kept. The clerk files your court papers and keeps the official records of your divorce. Most people who work in the clerk's office are friendly and helpful. While they can't give you legal advice (such as telling you what to say in your court papers), they can help explain the system and the procedures (such as telling you what type of papers must be filed). The clerk has the power to accept or reject your papers, so you don't want to anger the clerk either. If the clerk tells you to change something in your papers, just change it. Don't argue or complain.

Lawyers. Lawyers serve as guides through the legal system. They try to guide their own client, while trying to confuse, manipulate, or outmaneuver their opponent. In dealing with your spouse's lawyer (if he or she has one) try to be polite. You won't get anywhere by being antagonistic. Generally the lawyer is just doing his or her job to get the best situation for his client. Some lawyers are truly nasty people. These lawyers simply can't be reasoned with, and you shouldn't try. If your spouse gets one of these lawyers, it is a good idea for you to get a lawyer also. Chapter 3 will provide more information to help you decide if you want a lawyer.

This book. This book will serve as your map of the trail through the legal system. In most cases, the dangers along the way are relatively small. If you start getting lost, or the dangers seem to be getting worse, you can always hire a lawyer to jump to your aid.

THE LAW

The law relating to divorce, as well as to any other area of the law, comes from two sources. The first source is the General Statutes of North Carolina, which are the laws passed by the North Carolina Legislature. This book is designed so that you won't need to look up the law. However, a portion of the this law, relating to property division, alimony, and child support, can be found in appendix A of this book.

> **Residency Requirement:** One basic law you need to be aware of is that either you or your spouse must live in North Carolina for at least six months immediately before filing a complaint with the court.

The other source of law is the past decisions of the North Carolina courts. These are much more difficult to locate and follow. For most situations the law is clearly spelled out in the statutes, and the past court decisions are not all that important. However, if you wish to learn more about how to find these court decisions, see the section, LEGAL RESEARCH, on page 17.

The law is really very simple in most divorce cases. You will need to show the following three things:

1. That you have been separated for one year. (This is done simply by stating this fact, which means that for one year you lived in one place and your spouse lived in another.)

2. How your property should be divided between you and your spouse.

3. Who should have custody of your children and how they should be supported.

THE PROCEDURE

The basic uncontested divorce process may be viewed as a five-step process:

1. File court papers asking the judge to grant a divorce (which may include dividing your property and deciding how the children will be taken care of).

2. Notify your spouse that you are filing for divorce.

3. Schedule a hearing date.

4. Notify your spouse of the hearing date.

5. Attend the divorce hearing, and have the judge sign a judgment granting the divorce.

Now, we'll look at these steps in a little more detail, and later chapters will tell you how to carry out these steps.

Divorce Complaint. This is nothing more than a written request for the judge to grant you a divorce. Complaint forms are provided in appendix B of this book, and full instructions are also provided in later chapters. Once the complaint is completed, it is taken to the court clerk to be filed.

Notifying Your Spouse. After you've prepared the complaint you need to officially notify your spouse. Even though your spouse may already know that you are filing for divorce, you still need to have him or her officially notified. This is done by having a copy of your complaint delivered to your spouse. This must be done in a certain way, which will be explained in detail later.

Obtaining a Hearing Date. Once all of your paperwork is in order and has been filed and delivered to your spouse, you need to set a date for a hearing. A hearing is simply a meeting with the judge so that he or she can give you a divorce. Your spouse must be notified of the hearing date. The hearing can not be set for anytime prior to thirty days after your spouse received the divorce complaint. The hearing can sometimes be scheduled over the telephone. The clerk will be able to explain how to schedule a hearing.

The Hearing. Finally, you go to the divorce hearing. The judge will review the papers you have submitted, and any additional information you have, and will make a decision about whether to grant the divorce. If it applies to your situation, the judge will decide how much alimony you will receive, how your property should be divided, who should have custody of your children, and how the children are to be supported. However, each of these matters will be decided at a later time in separate hearings.

In some counties, the judge can order the husband and wife into mediation, when the parties are having a difficult time reaching agreement on the major issues. The judge can also direct the state Department of Social Services to conduct a study, and provide the judge with a custody recommendation.

Legal Research

This book has been designed so that you don't need to do legal research. However, if your case becomes complicated, or you simply have an interest in checking into the divorce law in North Carolina, this section will give you some guidance. There are two sources of law. One is the set of laws passed by the North Carolina Legislature. The other is the decisions of the courts in previous cases.

General Statutes of North Carolina

The main source of information on North Carolina divorce law is the *General Statutes of North Carolina*, which are found in numerous volumes. They contain the exact wording of each statute, followed by summaries (or *annotations*) of court cases that discuss each section of the statutes. For example, if you are looking for information about alimony, you would find Section 50-16.2. This would give you the exact language of the statute, that would be followed by summaries of court opinions explaining the alimony statute. (**Note:** Although the title on these volumes of books is General Statutes of North Carolina, they are more commonly referred to by lawyers and judges as "North Carolina General Statutes.")

The statutes are updated annually. A set can usually be found at the public library, although check to be sure they have the most recent set. You will primarily be concerned with Chapter 50 of the *General Statutes of North Carolina,* although you can look for other subjects in the index volume.

In addition to the laws passed by the legislature, law is also made by the decisions of the judges in various cases each year. To find this *case law* you will need to go to a law library. Each county has a law library connected with the court, so you can ask the court clerk where the library is located. Also, law schools have libraries that may be open to the public. Don't be afraid to ask the librarian for assistance. They cannot give you legal advice, but they can tell you where the books are located and they might even be kind enough to give you a short course on legal research. There are several types of books used to find the case law:

North Carolina Digest

The *North Carolina Digest* is a set of volumes that give short summaries of cases, and the place where you can find the court's full written opinion. The information in the digest is arranged alphabetically by subject. Find the chapter on "Divorce," then look for the headings of the subject you want.

Southeastern Reporter

The *Southeastern Reporter* is where the appeals courts publish their written opinions on the cases they hear. There are two *series* of the *Southeastern Reporter,* the older cases are compiled in the *Southeastern Reporter* (abbreviated "SE"), and newer cases compiled in the *Southeastern Reporter, 2d Series* (abbreviated "SE.2d"). For example, a typical reference in the digest might be: "*Smith v. Smith,* 149 SE 2d 721

(1994)." This tells you that the case of *Smith v. Smith* can be found by going to Volume 149 of the *Southeastern Reporter, 2d Series*, and turning to page 721. The number in parentheses (1994) tells you the case was decided by the court in the year 1994. In its opinion, the court will discuss what the case was about, what questions of law were presented for consideration, and what the court decided and why.

North Carolina Rules of Court

The *North Carolina Rules of Court* are the rules that are applied in the various courts in North Carolina, and they also contain some approved forms. These rules mainly deal with forms and procedures. You would be primarily concerned with the *Rules of Civil Procedure*.

Other Sources

Three other books you may want to ask for at the law library are:

- *Lee's North Carolina Law, 4th and 5th edition*, by Robert E. Lee, Suzanne Reynolds, Rhoda Billings, and Kenneth Craig (published by the Michie Company).
- *North Carolina Family and Related Laws Annotated, 1996 edition.*
- *Practical Family Law Desk and Form Book*, by the Wake Forest University Law School Continuing Legal Education Department.

You may also find other books on divorce law.

LAWYERS 3

Whether you need an attorney will depend upon many factors, such as how comfortable you feel handling the matter yourself, whether your situation is more complicated than usual, how much opposition you get from your spouse, and whether your spouse has an attorney. It may also be advisable to hire an attorney if you encounter a judge with a hostile attitude, or if your spouse gets a lawyer who wants to fight. There are no court appointed lawyers in divorce cases, so if you want an attorney you will have to hire one.

A very general rule is that you should consider hiring an attorney whenever you reach a point where you no longer feel comfortable representing yourself. This point will vary greatly with each person, so there is no easy way to be more definite.

A more appropriate question is: "Do you want a lawyer?" The next section will discuss some of the "pros" and "cons" of hiring a lawyer, and some of the things you may want to consider in making this decision.

DO YOU WANT A LAWYER?

One of the first questions you will want to consider, and most likely the reason you are reading this book, is: How much will an attorney cost?

Attorneys come in all ages, shapes, sizes, sexes, racial and ethnic groups, and price ranges. For a very rough estimate, you can expect an attorney to charge anywhere from $150 to $1,000 for an uncontested divorce, and from $800 and up for a contested divorce. Lawyers usually charge an hourly rate for contested divorces, ranging from about $75 to $300 per hour. Most new (and therefore less expensive) attorneys would be quite capable of handling a simple divorce, but if your situation became more complicated, you would probably prefer a more experienced lawyer.

Advantages to Hiring a Lawyer

The following are some reasons you may want to consider hiring a lawyer to represent you:

- Judges and other attorneys may take you more seriously. Most judges prefer both parties to have attorneys. They feel this helps the case move in a more orderly fashion, and both sides will know the procedures and relevant issues. Persons representing themselves very often waste a lot of time on matters that have absolutely no bearing on the outcome of the case.
- A lawyer will serve as a "buffer" between you and your spouse. This can lead to a quicker passage through the system, by reducing the chance for emotions to take control and confuse the issues.
- Attorneys prefer to deal with other attorneys, for the same reasons listed above. However, if you become familiar with this book, and conduct yourself in a calm and proper manner, you should have no trouble. (Proper courtroom manners will be discussed in a later chapter.)
- You can let your lawyer worry about all of the details. By having an attorney you need only become generally familiar with the contents of this book, as it will be your attorney's job to file the proper papers in the correct form, and to deal with the court clerks, the judge, the process server, your spouse, and your spouse's attorney.

- Lawyers provide professional assistance with legal problems. In the event your case is complicated, or suddenly becomes complicated, it is an advantage to have an attorney who is familiar with your case. It can also be comforting to have a lawyer to turn to for advice, and to get your questions answered.

Advantages to Representing Yourself

The following are some reasons you may want to represent yourself instead of hiring a lawyer:

- You save the cost of a lawyer.
- Sometimes judges feel more sympathetic toward a person not represented by an attorney. Sometimes this results in the unrepresented person being allowed a certain amount of leeway with the procedure rules.
- The procedure may be faster. Two of the most frequent complaints about lawyers received by the bar association involve delay in completing the case, and failure to return phone calls. Most lawyers have a heavy caseload, which sometimes results in cases being neglected for various periods of time. If you are following the progress of your own case you'll be able to push it along the system diligently.
- Selecting any attorney is not easy. As the next section shows, it is hard to know whether you are selecting an attorney you will be happy with.

Middle Ground

You may want to look for an attorney who will be willing to accept an hourly fee to answer your questions and give you help as you need it. This way you will save some legal costs, but still get some professional assistance.

Selecting a Lawyer

Selecting a lawyer is a two-step process. First you need to decide which attorney to make an appointment with, then you need to decide if you want to hire that attorney.

Finding Lawyers

To find a few lawyers from which you will make your eventual selection, consider the following sources:

- Ask a friend. A common, and frequently the best way to find a lawyer is to ask someone you know to recommend one to you. This is especially helpful if the lawyer represented your friend in a divorce, or other family law matter.
- Lawyer Referral Service. You can find a referral service by looking in the Yellow Pages phone directory under "Attorney Referral Services" or "Attorneys." This is a service, usually operated by a bar association, which is designed to match a client with an attorney handling cases in the area of law the client needs. The referral service does not guarantee the quality of work, nor the level of experience or ability, of the attorney. Finding a lawyer this way will at least connect you with one who is interested in divorce and family law matters, and probably has some experience in this area.
- Yellow Pages. Check under the heading for "Attorneys" in the Yellow Pages phone directory. Many of the lawyers and law firms will place display ads here indicating their areas of practice, and educational backgrounds. Look for firms or lawyers which indicate they practice in areas such as "divorce," "family law," or "domestic relations."
- Ask another Lawyer. If you have used the services of an attorney in the past for some other matter (for example, a real estate closing, traffic ticket, or a will), you may want to call and ask if he or she could refer you to an attorney whose ability in the area of family law is respected.

EVALUATING A LAWYER

From your search you should select three to five lawyers worthy of further consideration. Your first step will be to call each attorney's office, explain that you are interested in seeking a divorce, and ask the following questions:

- Does the attorney (or firm) handle this type of matter?
- How much can you expect it to cost? (Don't expect to get a definite answer, but it doesn't hurt to ask.)
- How soon can you get an appointment?

If you like the answers you get, ask if you can speak to the attorney. Some offices will permit this, but others will require you to make an appointment. Make the appointment if that is what is required. Once you get in contact with the attorney (either on the phone or at the appointment), ask the following questions:

- How much will it cost?
- How will the fee be paid?
- How long has the attorney been in practice?
- How long has the attorney been in practice in North Carolina?
- What percentage of the attorney's cases involve divorce cases or other family law matters? (Don't expect an exact answer, but you should get a rough estimate that is at least twenty percent.)
- How long will it take? (Don't expect an exact answer, but the attorney should be able to give you an average range and discuss things that may make a difference.)

If you get acceptable answers to these questions, it's time to ask yourself the following questions about the lawyer:

- Do you feel comfortable talking to the lawyer?
- Is the lawyer friendly toward you?
- Does the lawyer seem confident in himself or herself?

- Does the lawyer seem to be straight-forward with you, and able to explain things so you understand?

If you get satisfactory answers to all of these questions you probably have a lawyer you'll be able to work with. Most clients are happiest with an attorney they feel comfortable with.

Working With a Lawyer

In general, you will work best with your attorney if you keep an open, honest and friendly attitude. You should also consider the following suggestions.

Ask questions. If you want to know something or if you don't understand something, ask your attorney. If you don't understand the answer, tell your attorney and ask him or her to explain it again. There are many points of law that many lawyers don't fully understand, so you should not be embarrassed to ask questions. Many people who say they had a bad experience with a lawyer either didn't ask enough questions, or had a lawyer who wouldn't take the time to explain things to them. If your lawyer isn't taking the time to explain what he or she is doing, it may be time to look for a new lawyer.

Give your lawyer complete information. Anything you tell your attorney is confidential. An attorney can lose his license to practice if he reveals information without your permission. So don't hold back. Tell your lawyer everything, even if it doesn't seem important to you. There are many things that seem unimportant to a non-attorney, but can change the outcome of a case. Also, don't hold something back because you are afraid it will hurt your case. It will definitely hurt your case if your lawyer doesn't find out about it until he or she hears it in court from your spouse's attorney! But if your attorney knows in advance, he or she can plan to eliminate or reduce damage to your case.

Accept reality. Listen to what your lawyer tells you about the law and the system. It will do you no good to argue because the law or the system doesn't work the way you think it should. For example, if your lawyer tells you that the judge can't hear your case for two weeks, don't try demanding that he or she set a hearing tomorrow. By refusing to accept reality, you are only setting yourself up for disappointment. And remember: It's not your attorney's fault that the system isn't perfect, or that the law doesn't say what you'd like it to say.

Be patient. This applies to being patient with the system (which is often slow as we discussed earlier), as well as with your attorney. Don't expect your lawyer to return your phone call within an hour. He or she may not be able to return it the same day either. Most lawyers are very busy, and over-worked. It is rare that an attorney can maintain a full caseload and still make each client feel as if he or she is the only client.

Talk to the secretary. Your lawyer's secretary can be a valuable source of information. So be friendly and get to know him or her. Often the secretary will be able to answer your questions and you won't get a bill for the time you talk to him or her.

Let your attorney deal with your spouse. It is your lawyer's job to communicate with your spouse, or with your spouse's lawyer. Let your lawyer do his or her job. Many lawyers have had clients lose or damage their cases when the client decides to say or do something on their own.

Be on time. This applies to appointments with your lawyer, and to court hearings.

Keeping your case moving. Many lawyers operate on the old principle of "the squeaking wheel gets the oil." Work on a case tends to get put off until a deadline is near, an emergency develops, or the client calls. There is a reason for this. Many lawyers take more cases than can be effectively handled in order to obtain the income they desire. Your task is to become a squeaking wheel that doesn't squeak so much that you come to be considered a nuisance by the lawyer and his or her staff. Whenever you talk to your lawyer ask the following questions:

- What is the next step?
- When do you expect it to be done?
- When should I talk to you next?

If you don't hear from the lawyer when you expect, call him or her the following day. Don't remind your lawyer that he or she didn't call; just ask how things are going.

How to save money. Of course you don't want to spend unnecessary money for an attorney. Here are a few things you can do to avoid excess legal fees:

- Don't make unnecessary phone calls to your lawyer.
- Give information to the secretary whenever possible.
- Direct your question to the secretary first, who will refer it to the attorney if necessary.
- Plan your phone calls so you can get to the point, and take less of your attorney's time.
- Do some of the "leg work" yourself. Pick up and deliver papers yourself, for example. Ask your attorney what you can do to assist with your case.
- Be prepared for appointments. Have all related papers with you, plan your visit so that you get to the point, and make an outline of what you want to discuss and what questions you want to ask.

Pay your attorney bill when it's due. No client gets prompt attention like a client who pays his or her lawyer on time. However, you are entitled to an itemized bill, showing what the attorney did and how much time it took. Many attorneys will have you sign an agreement that states how you will be charged, what is included in the hourly fee, and what is extra. Review your bill carefully. There are numerous stories of people paying an attorney $500 or $1,000 in advance, only to have the attorney make a few phone calls to the spouse's lawyer, then ask for more money. If your attorney asks for $500 or $1,000 in advance, you should be sure that you and the lawyer agree on what is to be done for this fee. For $500 you should at least expect to have a petition prepared, filed with the court, and served on your spouse (although the filing and service fees will probably be extra).

Firing your lawyer. If you find that you can no longer work with your lawyer, or don't trust your lawyer, it is time to either go it alone or get a new attorney. You will need to send your lawyer a letter stating that you no longer desire his or her services, and are discharging him or her from your case. Also state that you will be coming by his or her office to pick up your file. The attorney does not have to give you his or her own notes or other work he or she has in progress, but your attorney must give you the essential contents of your file (such as copies of papers already filed or prepared and billed for, and any documents you provided). If your attorney refuses to give your file to you, contact the state bar association about filing a complaint, or *grievance,* against the lawyer. Of course, you will need to settle any remaining fees charged.

4 Do You Really Want a Divorce?

Getting a divorce is one of the most emotionally stressful events in a person's life. Only the death of one's child or spouse creates more stress than a divorce. It will also have an impact on several aspects of your life, and can change your entire lifestyle. Before you begin the process of getting a divorce, you need to take some time to think about how it will affect your life. This chapter will help you examine these things, and offer alternatives in the event you want to try to save your relationship. Even if you feel absolutely sure that you want a divorce, you should still read this chapter so you are prepared for what may follow.

Legal Divorce

In emotional terms, this is the easiest part of divorce. It is simply the breaking of your matrimonial bonds; the termination of your marriage contract and partnership. The stress created here is that of going through a court system procedure, and having to deal with your spouse as you go through it. However, when compared to the other aspects of divorce, the legal divorce doesn't last as long. On the other hand, the legal divorce can be the most confrontational and emotionally explosive stage.

There are generally three matters to be resolved through the legal divorce:

1. The divorce of two people: Basically, this gives each the legal right to marry someone else.
2. The division of their property (and responsibility for debts).
3. The care and custody of their children.

Although it is theoretically possible for the legal divorce to be concluded within a few months, the legalities most often continue for years. This is mostly caused by the emotional aspects leading to battles over the children.

Social and Emotional Divorce

Divorce will have a tremendous impact on your social and emotional lives, which will continue long after you are legally divorced. These impacts include:

Lack of companionship. Even if your relationship is quite "stormy," you are probably still accustomed to just having your spouse around. You may be able to temporarily put aside your problems, and at least somewhat support each other in times of mutual adversity (such as in dealing with a death in the family, the illness of your child, or hurricane damage to your home). You may also just feel a little more secure at night, just not being alone in the house. Even if your marriage is one of the most miserable, you may still notice at least a little emptiness, loneliness, or solitude after the divorce. It may not be that you miss your spouse in particular, but just miss another person being around.

Grief. Divorce may be viewed as the death of a marriage, or maybe the funeral ceremony for the death of a marriage. And like the death of anyone or anything you've been close to, you will feel a sense of loss. This aspect can take you through all of the normal feelings associated with grief, such as guilt, anger, denial, and acceptance. You'll get angry and frustrated over the years you've "wasted." You'll feel guilty because you "failed to make the marriage work." You'll find yourself saying, "I can't believe this is happening to me." And, for months or even years, you'll spend a lot of time thinking about your marriage. It can be extremely difficult to put it all behind you, and to get on with your life.

The single's scene: dating. After divorce, your social life will change. If you want to avoid solitary evenings before the TV, you'll find yourself trying to get back into the "single's scene." This will probably involve a change in friends, as well as a change in life-style. First, you may find that your current friends, who are probably all married, no longer find you, as a single person, fit in with their circle. Gradually, or even quickly, you may find yourself dropped from their guest list. Now you've got to start making an effort to meet single people at work, going out on the town, and even dating! This experience can be very frightening, tiring, and frustrating after years of being away from this life-style. It can also be very difficult if you have custody of the kids. And the dating scene is (or at least should be) entirely changed with the ever-present threat of AIDS and other communicable diseases.

Financial Divorce

This can be a very long and drastic adjustment. Divorce has a significant financial impact in just about every case. Many married couples are just able to make ends meet. After getting divorced there are suddenly two rent payments, two electric bills, etc. For the spouse without custody, there is also child support to be paid. For at least one spouse, and often for both, money becomes even tighter than it was before the divorce. Also, once you've divided your property, each of you will need to replace the items the other person got to keep. If she got the bedroom furniture and the pots and pans, he will need to buy his own. If he got the TV and the sofa, she will need to buy her own TV and sofa.

Children and Divorce

The effect upon your children, and your relationship with them, can often be the most painful and long-lasting aspect of divorce. Your family life will be permanently changed, as there will no longer be the "family." Even if you remarry, step-parents rarely bring back that same family feeling. Your relationship with your children may become strained as they work through their feelings of blame, guilt, disappointment, and anger. This strain may continue for many years. Your children may even need professional counseling. Also, as long as there is child support and visitation involved, you will be forced to have at least some contact with your ex-spouse.

Alternatives to Divorce

By the time you've purchased this book, and read this far, you have probably already decided that you want a divorce. However, if what you've just read and thought about has changed your mind, or made you want to make a last effort to save your marriage, there are a few things you can try. These are only very basic suggestions. Details, and other suggestions, can be offered by professional marriage counselors.

Talk to Your Spouse

Choose the right time (not when your spouse is trying to unwind after a day at work, or is trying to quiet a screaming baby), and talk about your problems. Try to establish a few ground rules for the discussion, such as:

- Talk about how you feel, instead of making accusations that may start an argument.
- Each person listens while the other speaks (no interrupting).
- Each person must say something that he or she likes about the other, and about the relationship.

As you talk you may want to discuss such things as where you'd like your relationship to go, how it has changed since you got married, and what can be done to bring you closer together.

Change Your Thinking

Many people get divorced because they won't change something about their outlook or their lifestyle. Then, once they get divorced, they find they've made that same change they resisted for so long.

For example, George and Wendy were unhappy in their marriage. They didn't seem to share the same lifestyle. George felt overburdened with responsibility and bored. He wanted Wendy to be more independent and outgoing, to meet new people, to handle the household budget, and to go out with him more often. But Wendy was more shy and reserved, wasn't confident in her ability to find a job and succeed in the business world, and preferred to stay at home. Wendy wanted George to give up some of his frequent nights "out with the guys," to help with the cooking and laundry, to stop leaving messes for her to clean up, and to stop bothering her about going out all the time. But neither would try change, and eventually all of the little things built up into a divorce.

After the divorce, Wendy was forced to get a job to support herself. Now she's made friends at work, she goes out with them two or three nights a week, she's successful and happy at her job, and she's quite competent at managing her own budget. George now has his own apartment, and has to cook his own meals (something he finds he enjoys), and do his own laundry. He's also found it necessary to clean up his own messes and keep the place neat, especially if he's going to entertain guests. George has even thought about inviting Wendy over for dinner and a quiet evening at his place. Wendy has been thinking about inviting George out for a drink after work with her friends.

Both George and Wendy have changed in exactly the way the other had wanted. It's just too bad they didn't make these changes before they got divorced! If you think some change may help, give it a try. You can always go back to a divorce if things don't work out.

Counseling

Counseling is not the same as giving advice. A counselor should not be telling you what to do. A counselor's job is to assist you in figuring out what you really want to do. A counselor's job is mostly to ask questions that will get you thinking.

Actually, just talking things out with your spouse is a form of self-counseling. The only problem is that it's difficult to remain objective and non-judgmental. You both need to be able to calmly analyze what the problems are, and discuss possible solutions. Very few couples seem to be able to do this successfully, which is why there are professional marriage counselors. As with doctors and lawyers, good marriage counselors are best discovered by word of mouth. You may have friends who can direct you to someone who helped them. You can also check with your family doctor or your clergyman for a referral, or even check the telephone Yellow Pages under "Marriage and Family Counselors" or some similar category. You can see a counselor either alone or with your spouse. It may be a good idea to see a counselor even if you are going through with the divorce.

Another form of individual counseling is talking to a close friend. Just remember the difference between counseling and advice giving! Don't let your friend tell you what you should do.

Trial Separation

Before going through the time, expense, and trouble of getting a divorce, you and your spouse may want to try just getting away from each other for awhile. This can be as simple as taking separate vacations, or as complex as actually separating into separate households for an indefinite period of time.

This may give each of you a chance to think about how you'll like living alone, how important or trivial your problems are, and how you really feel about each other. Talk about how you feel, instead of making accusations that may start an argument.

5 Evaluating Your Situation

This book assumes that you and your spouse are already separated. North Carolina law requires that you be separated for more than one year before you file for divorce. The following things should be done or considered before you begin the divorce process.

Your Spouse

First, you need to evaluate your situation with respect to your spouse. Have you both already agreed to get a divorce? If not, what kind of reaction do you expect from him or her? Your expected reaction can determine how you proceed. If he or she reacts in a rational manner, you can probably use the standard or uncontested procedure. But if you expect an extremely emotional and possibly violent reaction, you will need to take steps to protect yourself, your children, and your property; and will have to anticipate using the contested procedure.

You were warned on the back cover of this book not to let your spouse find this book, and it was for a very good reason. Unless you and your spouse have already decided together to get a divorce, you don't want your spouse to know you are thinking about filing for divorce. This is a defense tactic, although it may not seem that way at first. If your spouse thinks you are planning a divorce, he or she may do things to prevent you from getting a fair result. These things include withdrawing money from bank accounts, hiding information about income, and hiding assets. So don't let on until you've collected all of the information you will need and are about to file with the court, or until you are prepared to protect yourself from violence, if necessary.

Caution: Tactics such as withdrawing money from bank accounts and hiding assets are dangerous. If you try any of these things you risk looking like the "bad guy" before the judge. This can result in anything from having disputed matters resolved in your spouse's favor, to being ordered to produce the assets (or be jailed for contempt of court).

Theoretically, the "system" would prefer you to keep evidence of the assets (such as photographs, sales receipts, or bank statements), to present to the judge if your spouse hides them. Then your spouse will be the bad guy and risk being jailed. However, once your spouse has taken assets, and hidden them, or sold them and spent the money, even a contempt order may not get the money or assets back. If you determine that you need to get the assets in order to keep your spouse from hiding or disposing of them, be sure you keep them in a safe place, and disclose them on your FINANCIAL AFFIDAVIT (Form 15). Do not dispose of them. If your spouse claims you took them, you can explain to the judge why you were afraid that your spouse would dispose of them and that you merely got them out of his or her reach.

GATHERING INFORMATION

It is extremely important that you collect all of the financial information you can get. This information should include originals or copies of the following:

1. Your most recent income tax return (and your spouse's if you filed separately).

2. The most recent W-2 tax forms for yourself and your spouse.
3. Any other income reporting papers (such as interest, stock dividends, etc.).
4. Your spouse's most recent paystub, hopefully showing year-to-date earnings (otherwise try to get copies of all paystubs since the beginning of the year).
5. Deeds to all real estate; and car, boat, or other vehicle titles.
6. Your and your spouse's will.
7. Life insurance policies.
8. Stocks, bonds, or other investment papers.
9. Pension or retirement fund papers and statements.
10. Health insurance card and papers.
11. Bank account or credit union statements.
12. Your spouse's social security number, and driver's license number.
13. Names, addresses, and phone numbers of your spouse's employer, close friends, and family members.
14. Credit card statements, mortgage documents, and other credit and debt papers.
15. A list of vehicles, furniture, appliances, tools, etc., owned by you and your spouse. (See the next section in this chapter on PROPERTY AND DEBTS for forms and a detailed discussion of what to include.)
16. Copies of bills or receipts for recurring, regular expenses, such as electric, gas or other utilities, car insurance, etc.
17. Copies of bills, receipts, insurance forms, or medical records for any unusual medical expenses (including for recurring or continuous medical conditions) for yourself, your spouse, or your children.

18. Any other papers showing what you and your spouse earn, own or owe.

Make copies of as many of these papers as possible, and keep them in a safe and private place (where your spouse won't find them). Try to make copies of new papers as they come in, especially as you get close to filing court papers, and as you get close to a court hearing.

Property and Debts

This section is designed to help you get a rough idea of where things stand regarding the division of your property and debts, and to prepare you for completing the court papers you will need to file. The following sections will deal with the questions of child support, custody, and visitation. If you are still not sure whether you want a divorce, these sections may help you to decide.

Asset and Debt Division Under North Carolina Law

Trying to determine how to divide assets and debts can be difficult. Under North Carolina's *equitable distribution* law assets and debts are separated into two categories: *marital* (meaning it is both yours and your spouse's), and *separate* (meaning it is yours or your spouse's alone). In making this distinction the following rules apply:

1. If the asset or debt was acquired after the date you were married and before you separated, it is presumed to be a marital asset or debt. It is up to you or your spouse to prove otherwise.

2. In order to be a separate asset or debt, it must have been acquired before the date of marriage or after the date of separation. Also, it is separate if you acquired it through a gift or inheritance (as long as it wasn't a gift from your spouse), and this includes income from separate property. (Example: rent you receive from an investment property you had before you got married. If you exchange one of these assets or debts after your marriage, it is still separate. Example: you had a $6,000 car before you got married. After the

marriage, you traded it for a different $6,000 car.) Finally, you and your spouse may sign a written agreement that certain assets and debts are to be considered separate.

3. Marital assets and debts are those that were acquired during your marriage, even if they were acquired by you or your spouse individually. This also includes the increase in value of a separate asset during the marriage, or due to the use of marital funds to pay for or improve property. All rights accrued during the marriage in pension, retirement, profit-sharing, insurance and similar plans are marital assets. It is also possible for one spouse to make a gift of separate property to the other spouse, thereby making it marital property.

4. Real estate that is in both names is considered marital property, and it's up to the spouse claiming otherwise to prove it.

5. Finally, whether an asset or debt is marital or separate, and the value of any asset is determined as of the date of separation.

PROPERTY

This section is designed to help you get a rough idea of where things stand regarding the division of your property, and to prepare you for completing the court papers you will need to file. The following sections will deal with the questions of your debts, child support, custody, and visitation. If you are still not sure whether you want a divorce, these sections may help you to decide.

This section basically assists you in completing the PROPERTY INVENTORY (Form 1 in appendix B of this book). This form is a list of all of your property, and key information about that property. You will notice that this form is divided into nine columns, designated as follows:

Column (1): You will check the box in this column if that piece of property is separate property. This is property that either you or your spouse acquired before you were married, or which were given to you or your spouse separately, or which were inherited by you or your spouse separately. (See appendix A, Section 50-20 of the General Statutes of North Carolina for a detailed explanation of marital and separate assets and liabilities.)

Column (2): In this column you will describe the property. A discussion regarding what information should go in this column will follow.

Column (3): This column is used to write in the serial number, account number, or other number that will help clearly identify that piece of property.

Column (4): This is for the current market value of the property.

Column (5): This will show how much money is owed on the property, if any.

Column (6): Subtract the BALANCE OWED from the VALUE. This will show how much the property is worth to you (your EQUITY).

Column (7): This column will show the current legal owner of the property. (H) designates the husband, (W) the wife, and (J) is for jointly owned property (in both of your names).

Column (8): This column will be checked for those pieces of property you expect the husband will keep.

Column (9): This column is for the property you expect the wife will keep.

Use columns (1) through (7) to list your property, including the following:

Cash. List the name of the bank, credit union, etc., and the account number, for each account. This includes savings and checking accounts, and certificates of deposit (CDs). The balance of each account should be listed in the columns entitled VALUE and EQUITY (Leave the BALANCE OWED column blank.) Make copies of the most recent bank statements for each account.

Stocks and bonds. All stocks, bonds, or other "paper investments" should be listed. Write down the number of shares and the name of the company or other organization that issued them. Also copy any notation such as "common" or "preferred" stock or shares. This information can be obtained from the stock certificate itself, or from a statement from the stock broker. Make a copy of the certificate or the statement.

Real estate. List each piece of property you and your spouse own. The description might include a street address for the property, a subdivision name, and lot number, or anything that lets you know what piece of property you are referring to. There probably won't be an ID number, although you might use the county's tax number. Real estate (or any other property) may be in both of your names (joint), in your spouse's name alone, or in your name alone. The only way to know for sure is to look at the deed to the property. (If you can't find a copy of the deed, try to find mortgage papers or payment coupons, homeowners insurance papers, or a property tax assessment notice.) The owners of property are usually referred to on the deed as the *grantees*. In assigning a value to the property, consider the market value, which is how much you could probably sell the property for. This might be what similar houses in your neighborhood have sold for recently. You might also consider how much you paid for the property, or how much the property is insured for. *Do not* use the tax assessment value, as this is usually considerably lower than the market value.

Vehicles. This category includes cars, trucks, motor homes, recreational vehicles (RVs), motorcycles, boats, trailers, airplanes, and any other means of transportation for which the State requires a title and registration. Your description should include the following information (which can usually be found on the title or on the vehicle itself):

- Year it was made.
- Make: The name of the manufacturer, such as "Ford," "Honda," "Chris Craft," etc.
- Model: You know it's a Ford, but is it a Mustang, an LTD, or an Aerostar: The model may be a name, a number, a series of letters, or a combination of these.
- Serial Number: This is most likely found on the vehicle, as well as on the title or registration.

Make a copy of the title or registration. Regarding a value, you can go to the public library and ask to look at a *blue book* for cars, trucks or whatever it is you're looking for. A blue book (which may actually be yellow, black, or any other color) gives the average values for used vehicles. Your librarian can help you find what you need. Another source is to look in the classified advertising section of a newspaper to see what similar vehicles are selling for. You might also try calling a dealer to see if he can give you a rough idea of the value. Be sure you take into consideration the condition of the vehicle.

Furniture. List all furniture as specifically as possible. Include the type of piece (such as sofa, coffee table, etc.), the color, and if you know it, the manufacturer, line name, or the style. Furniture usually won't have a serial number, although if you find one be sure to write it on the list. Just estimate a value, unless you just know what it's worth.

Appliances, electronic equipment, and yard machines. This category includes such things as refrigerators, lawn mowers, and power tools. Again, estimate a value, unless you are familiar enough with them to simply know what they are worth. There are too many different makes, models, accessories, and age factors to be able to figure out a value otherwise. These items will probably have a make, model, and serial number on them. You may have to look on the back, bottom, or other hidden place for the serial number, but try to find it.

Jewelry and other valuables. You don't need to list inexpensive, or costume jewelry. And you can plan on keeping your own personal watches, rings, etc. However, if you own an expensive piece you should include it in your list, along with an estimated value. Be sure to include silverware, original art, gold, coin collections, etc. Again, be as detailed and specific as possible.

Life insurance with cash surrender value. This is any life insurance policy which you may cash in or borrow against, and therefore has value. If you can't find a cash surrender value in the papers you have, you can call the insurance company and ask.

Other "big ticket" items. This is simply a general reference to anything of significant value that doesn't fit in one of the categories already discussed. Examples might be a portable spa, an above-ground swimming pool, golf clubs, guns, pool tables, camping or fishing equipment, or farm animals or machinery.

Pensions and military benefits. The division of pensions, and military and retirement benefits, can be a complicated matter. Whenever these types of benefits are involved, you will need to consult an attorney or a CPA to determine the value of the benefits and how they should be divided. Be sure to read the section in chapter 13 on pension plans.

What not to list. You will not need to list your clothing and other personal effects. Pots, pans, dishes, and cooking utensils ordinarily do not need to be listed, unless they have some unusually high value.

Once you have completed your list, go back through it and try to determine who should end up with each item. The ideal situation is for both you and your spouse to go through the list together, and divide things fairly. However, if this is not possible, you will need to offer a reasonable settlement to the judge. Consider each item, and make a checkmark in either column (8) or (9) to designate whether that item should go to the husband or wife. You may make the following assumptions:

- Your separate property will go to you.

- Your spouse's separate property will go to your spouse.
- You should get the items that only you use.
- Your spouse should get the items only used by your spouse.
- The remaining items should be divided, evening out the total value of all the marital property, and taking into consideration who would really want that item.

To somewhat equally divide your property (we're only talking about marital property here), you first need to know what the total value of your property is. First of all, do not count the value of the separate items. Add the remaining amounts in the EQUITY column of Form 1, which will give you an approximate value of all marital property.

When it comes time for the hearing, you and your spouse may be arguing over some or all of the items on your list. This is when you'll be glad that you made copies of the documents relating to the property on your list. Arguments over the value of property may need to be resolved by hiring appraisers to set a value; however, you'll have to pay the appraiser a fee. Dividing your property will be discussed further in later chapters. (See chapter 9 for information on dividing property in contested cases.)

Debts

This section relates to the Debt Inventory (Form 2 in appendix B of this book), which will list your debts. Although there are cases where, for example, the wife gets a car but the husband is ordered to make the payments, generally whoever gets the property also gets the debt owed on that property. This seems to be a fair arrangement in most cases. On Form 2 you will list each debt owed by you or your spouse. As with separate property, there is also separate debt. This is any debt incurred before you were married, that is yours alone. Form 2 contains a column for "S" debts, which should be checked for each separate debt. You will be responsible for your separate debts, and your spouse will be responsible for his or hers.

To complete the DEBT INVENTORY (Form 2), list each debt as follows:

Column (1): Check if this is a separate debt. (See appendix A, Section 50-20 of the General Statutes of North Carolina, for a detailed explanation of marital and separate assets and debts.)

Column (2): Write in the name and address of the creditor (i.e., the bank, company, or person to whom the debt is owed).

Column (3): Write in the account, loan, or mortgage number.

Column (4): Write in any notes to help identify what the loan was for, such as "Christmas gifts," "Vacation," etc.

Column (5): Write in the monthly payment amount.

Column (6): Write in the balance still owed on the loan.

Column (7): Write in the date (approximately) when the loan was made.

Column (8): Note whether the account is in the husband's name (H), the wife's name (W), or jointly in both names (J).

Columns (9) & (10): These columns are to note who will be responsible for the debt after the divorce. As with your property, each of you will keep your separate debts, and the remainder should be divided, taking into consideration who will keep the property the loan was incurred for and equally dividing the overall debt. (See chapter 9 for information on dividing debts in contested cases.)

CHILD CUSTODY AND VISITATION

As with everything else in divorce, things are ideal when both parties can agree on the question of custody of the children. Generally, the judge will accept any agreement you reach, provided it doesn't appear that your agreement will cause harm to your children.

North Carolina child custody law can be put into one basic principle:

> *Between the mother and father, whether natural or adoptive, no presumption shall apply as to who will better promote the interest and welfare of the child.*

In spite of this modern philosophy voiced by the North Carolina legislature, you will find most judges are from the old school of thought on this subject and believe that (all things being equal) a young child is better off with the mother. Because of this statement in the law the judge may go to great lengths to find that all things are not equal, so as to justify his decision to award custody to the mother. It happens day after day throughout the state, and it's a reality you have to deal with.

Although, they are not bound by law to do so most courts tend to favor custody arrangements that allow for parents to share responsibility. This arrangement is commonly known as *joint custody*. While it is a great idea in its concept, it is usually not a very practical one. Very few parents can put aside their anger to each other to agree on what is best for their child. Joint custody merely leads to more fighting. And even if joint custody is ordered, a child can only have one primary residence. So the judge may still decide which parent the child will mainly live with, as well as how decisions regarding such things as education, and medical and dental care will be made.

If you and your spouse cannot agree on how these matters will be handled, you will be leaving this important decision up to the judge. The judge cannot possibly know your child as well as you and your spouse, so doesn't it make sense for you to work this out yourselves? Otherwise you are leaving the decision to a stranger.

If the judge must decide the question, he will consider the following factors:

- Which parent is most likely to allow the other to visit with the child.
- The love, affection and other emotional ties existing between the child and each parent.
- The ability and willingness of each parent to provide the child with food, clothing, medical care, and other material needs.
- The length of time the child has lived with either parent in a stable environment.
- The permanence, as a family unit, of the proposed custodial home. (This relates to where one of the parties will be getting remarried immediately after the divorce or, more often, to change of custody petitions at a later date.)
- The moral fitness of each parent.
- The mental and physical health of each parent.
- The home, school, and community record of the child.
- The preference of the child, providing the child is of sufficient intelligence and understanding.
- Any other fact the judge decides is relevant.

It is difficult to predict the outcome of a custody battle. There are too many factors and individual circumstances to make such a guess. The only exception is where one parent is clearly unfit and the other can prove it. Drug abuse is probably the most common charge against a spouse, but unless there has been an arrest and conviction it is difficult to prove to a judge. In general, don't charge your spouse with being unfit unless you can prove it. Judges are not impressed with unfounded allegations, and they can do more harm than good.

If your children are older (not infants), it may be a good idea to seriously consider their preference for with whom they would like to live. Your fairness and respect for their wishes may benefit you in the long run. Just be sure to keep in close contact with them and visit with them often.

Child Support

Once again the judge will probably go along with any agreement you and your spouse reach, as long as he is satisfied that the child will be adequately taken care of. The following information, and the North Carolina Child Support Guidelines, found in appendix A of this book, will help you get an idea of the proper amount of child support.

Child Support Forms

Forms 3, 4, and 5 are child support worksheets. You will need to select the worksheet that corresponds with your custody arrangement. If you and your spouse have an arrangement where one of you will have sole custody then use WORKSHEET A—CHILD SUPPORT OBLIGATION—SOLE CUSTODY (Form 3). For joint or shared custodial arrangements use WORKSHEET B—CHILD SUPPORT OBLIGATION—JOINT OR SHARED PHYSICAL CUSTODY (Form 4). For split custody arrangements use WORKSHEET C—CHILD SUPPORT OBLIGATION—SPLIT CUSTODY (Form 5).

The Child Support Guidelines in appendix A contain instructions on when each form should be used. Because you may need to file the worksheet with the court, make a copy of it to use now. On the back of each worksheet you will find instructions to help you fill in the information required.

You are only trying to get a rough idea of the amount of child support to expect. Later, after you have more accurate income information, you will complete the copy to file with the court clerk. As you prepare your form to file, you will refer back to this section for instructions in completing this form.

Even if you and your spouse can agree on a support amount, it should be close to the guidelines amount. The guidelines use the following procedure [for illustrative purposes we will be using WORKSHEET A—CHILD SUPPORT OBLIGATION—SOLE CUSTODY (Form 3)]:

HOW CHILD SUPPORT IS DETERMINED

Generally there are two factors used to determine the proper amount of support to be paid: 1) the needs of the child, and 2) the financial ability of each parent to meet those needs. North Carolina has simplified this procedure by clearly establishing a formula to be used in calculating both the needs of the child and each parent's ability to meet those needs. In filling out the worksheet be sure to convert everything to monthly amounts. The following steps are used in determining the proper amount of support:

1. You and your spouse each provide proof of your *gross income*.
2. Your *adjusted gross incomes* are determined by subtracting any preexisting child support payments and responsibility for other children.
3. Your adjusted gross incomes are added together to arrive at your *combined income*.
4. The adjusted gross income of each parent is divided by the combined income. This gives each parent's percentage of the combined income.
5. The combined income and the number of children you have are used to establish the children's needs, which is called the *basic child support obligation*. (This is done by reading a chart, a copy of which may be found in appendix A as part of the Child Support Guidelines.) It is important to note that if the income of the parent without custody falls within the shaded area of the chart, you should use that parent's adjusted gross income rather than your combined income to determine the basic child support obligation.
6. Make any necessary adjustments to the basic child support obligation by adding work related child care costs, health insurance premiums, and extraordinary expenses to the basic child support obligation. This gives you the total child support obligation.

7. The non-custodial parent's percentage, from step four above, is multiplied by the total child support obligation.

8. Then, subtract the amount of the adjustment the parent without custody is paying for work related child care costs, health insurance premiums and extraordinary expenses to determine their child support obligation.

This procedure can be used by most people. However, if you and your spouse's combined income is more than $15,000 per month, these guidelines aren't used. These guidelines will be discussed more below, and their complete text can be found in appendix A of this book.

> **Caution:** These are basic guidelines to a typical, simple situation. The calculation of child support can become complicated in certain situations. To more fully understand child support calculations, and to become aware of what special circumstances may affect the calculation, be sure to read the entire child support guidelines in appendix A, and the information and instructions on the back of the worksheet you use.

Income Determination

Gross Income. The first thing you will need to do is determine your gross income. This is basically your income before any deductions for taxes, social security, etc. The following money sources are considered part of gross income:

- Salary or wages.
- Overtime, commissions, bonuses, allowances, tips, etc.
- Business income from self-employment, partnerships, corporations, and independent contracts (gross receipts, minus ordinary and necessary expenses).
- Disability benefits.
- Workers' Compensation.

- Unemployment Compensation.
- Pension, retirement, or annuity payments.
- Social security benefits.
- Alimony received from a previous marriage.
- Interest and dividends.
- Rental income (gross receipts, minus ordinary and necessary expenses, but not depreciation).
- Income from royalties, trusts, or estates

You would fill in the total income from each of these sources for you and your spouse on line 1 of the WORKSHEET.

If you voluntarily reduce your income, or quit your job, the judge can refuse to recognize the reduction or loss of income. This is *imputed income*. The only exception may be where you are required to take such an action to stay home and care for your child. If this question comes up, the judge will decide whether you need to stay home, so be ready to explain your reasons.

Adjusted Gross Income. Adjusted gross income is determined by subtracting certain deductions from your gross income. The following deductions are allowed:

- Court-ordered support for other children (but only if you are actually paying it).
- Responsibility for other children. There may be an adjustment due to the financial responsibility a parent has for children who reside in his or her household, but who are not subjects of the child support order. (For more information about this, see the instructions in the Child Support Guidelines and on the back of the child support worksheets.)

Your gross income minus these deductions will give you your adjusted gross income. The same process should be applied to your spouse's income to arrive at his or her adjusted gross income. Fill in the allowable deductions for yourself and your spouse where indicated on the WORKSHEET. Now, subtract the total deductions from the gross income (line 1), and write the answers in line 2. This gives you your adjusted gross incomes.

Combined Income. Combined income is simply your adjusted gross income added to your spouse's adjusted gross income. For example: Your adjusted gross income is $1200 per month. Your spouse's adjusted gross income is $1800 per month. Your combined income is $3000 (1200 + 1800). Add your adjusted gross income and your spouse's adjusted gross income from line 2, and write the answer in the space provided. This is your combined income.

CALCULATING CHILD SUPPORT

The next step is to determine each parent's percentage share of their combined income. To get your share, divide your adjusted gross income by the combined income (1200 divided by 3000). The answer is .4. Next divide your spouse's adjusted gross income by the combined income (1800 divided by 3000). The answer is .6. Write in these percentages on line 3.

Once you determine each parents percentage share of their combined income, turn to the child support guidelines table in appendix A (this chart comes from Section 50-13.4 of the General Statutes of North Carolina). Read down the first column to your combined income, then read across to the column for the number of children for which support is owed. This figure will give you the needs of your children. Write in the needs indicated by the support table for your children in line 4.

Next, write in the amount of work related child care costs, health insurance premium paid for the children, and extraordinary expenses that are paid by both you and your spouse in the appropriate columns on lines 5a, 5b, and 5c. Combine the total adjustments on the appropriate column in line 5d.

Add the amount on line 4 to the total adjustments on line 5d and enter the total on line 6. Then multiply the percentage on line 3 (for the parent without custody) by the amount on line 6. Next, enter the total adjustments for the parent without custody on line 8, then subtract that amount from the amount on line 7. This will give you the child support obligation for the parent without custody.

Again using our example: We've established that your combined income is $3000 per month. Find the figure "3000" in the left column, then read across for the number of children. For one child the needs are $517 per month; for two children the needs are $749; for three children the needs are $881 etc. For our example, let's assume you have two children, so their monthly needs are $749.

Next, determine the necessary adjustments by calculating the total amount each parent pays for work related child care costs, health insurance premiums, and extraordinary expenses. For purposes of this example, let's assume each parent has $100 in adjustments. Add the total adjustment to the basic child support obligation ($749 + $200 = $949) to determine the total child support obligation.

Next, multiply the total child support obligation by your percentage share ($949 x .4 = $379.60). Now multiply the total child support obligation by your spouse's percentage share ($949 x .6 = $569.40). To determine the amount of support you will be expected to contribute, subtract the amount of your adjustments ($379.60 - $100 = $279.60). To determine the amount of support your spouse will be expected to contribute, subtract the amount of his or her adjustment ($569.40 - $100 = $469.40). Whichever parent does not have custody will be ordered to pay support according to this calculation. In our example, if you have custody, your spouse will be ordered to pay $469.40 per month. If your spouse has custody, you will be ordered to pay $279.60 per month. Write the contributions of you and your spouse on line 9.

There are some factors that may change the amount of support ordered according to the guidelines explained above. In some instances, the judge has the discretion to adjust the child support obligation to reflect the existence of any extraordinary expenses. These expenses might include extraordinary medical expenses, transportation costs or educational needs. The judge can also deviate from the guidelines if the amount of child support is unjust because it would not meet or would exceed the needs of the children. If any of these factors apply to your situation you may need the assistance of an attorney in persuading the judge to deviate from the guidelines.

Alimony

In 1995, the North Carolina Legislature changed the laws governing alimony. The major change provided that fault on behalf of the supporting spouse is no longer a precondition to getting alimony. Fault is now only a factor the court can consider.

North Carolina law provides that alimony may be granted to either husband or wife. (See appendix A, Sections 50-16.1A, 50-16.2A and 50-16.3A of the General Statutes of North Carolina, for a detailed explanation of the factors involved in deciding the issue of alimony.) Alimony can be awarded for an extended period (permanent) or temporarily while the divorce is pending (called *postseparation support*).

In general, in order for a spouse to receive alimony he or she must show the following: (1) that he or she was the *dependent spouse*; and (2) that the opposing spouse was the *supporting spouse* (these terms are defined in section 50-16.1A of the General Statutes of North Carolina). Then, the court must consider all relevant factors and make a finding that an award of alimony is equitable under the circumstances.

The most common factor courts consider in determining whether awarding alimony is equitable (and the amount and duration of the award) is marital misconduct of either spouse. It is important to note that the court will not award alimony to a spouse guilty of marital misconduct.

Marital misconduct includes the following:

1. Illicit sexual behavior such as, adultery and unnatural sex acts.
2. Involuntary separation due to one spouse's criminal conduct.
3. Abandonment.
4. Cruel and barbarous treatment.
5. Maliciously turning the other spouse out of doors.
6. Committing indignities that renders the other spouse's life intolerable.
7. Reckless spending of the other spouse's income.
8. Excessive use of drugs or alcohol.
9. Willful failure to provide subsistence according to one's means.

The other factors the court will consider in determining the equity of an alimony award include the following:

1. The relative earnings and earning capacity of each spouse.
2. The age, physical, mental, and emotional condition of each spouse.
3. The amount and sources of unearned income of both spouses.
4. The duration of the marriage.
5. The contribution by one spouse to the education, training, or increased earning power of the other spouse.
6. The extent to which the earning power, expenses, or financial obligations will be affected by reason of serving as the custodian of a minor child.
7. The standard of living established during the marriage.
8. The relative education of each spouse.
9. The relative debt and other financial obligations of each spouse.
10. The amount of property each spouse brought to the marriage.
11. The contribution of a spouse as homemaker.

12. The relative needs of the spouses.
13. The tax consequences of an alimony award.
14. Any other factor the judge finds necessary for a fair result.

As an alternative to alimony, you may want to try to negotiate to receive (or give up) a greater percentage of the property instead. This may be less of a hassle in the long run, but it may change the tax consequences of your divorce. (See chapter 12, regarding taxes.)

> **Note:** If you wish to obtain alimony or equitable distribution you must request it prior to the entry of your divorce decree.

Which Procedure to Use

Technically, there is only one divorce procedure. However, for clarification we will refer to three. These three are:

1. Standard divorce procedure;
2. Uncontested divorce procedure; and
3. Contested divorce procedure.

These procedures use the same set of forms, but are treated as separate procedures because they each require different information, and the steps vary with each procedure.

Chapter 7 of this book describes the standard divorce procedure, chapter 8 describes the uncontested divorce procedure, and chapter 9 describes the contested divorce procedure. You should read this entire book once before you begin filling out any court forms.

Residency Requirement

> **Caution:** Before you can use any procedure you or your spouse must have lived in North Carolina for at least six months before filing your divorce complaint.

STANDARD DIVORCE PROCEDURE

If you can answer "No" to all three of the following questions, you should follow the steps outlined in the standard divorce procedure:

1. Do you and your spouse have minor children?
2. Do you and your spouse own any major assets?
3. Do you want to obtain alimony?

UNCONTESTED DIVORCE PROCEDURE

If your situation does not fall within the guidelines for the standard procedure, you will have to use the uncontested procedure or contested procedure. The uncontested procedure should be used by those who are in agreement (or can reach an agreement) about how to divide the property and about who should have custody. It is similar to the standard procedure, although additional forms are needed.

CONTESTED DIVORCE PROCEDURE

The contested procedure will be necessary where you and your spouse are arguing over some matter, and can't resolve it. This may be the result of disagreement over custody of the children, the payment of child support or alimony, the division of your property, or any combination of these items. The section of this book dealing with the contested procedure builds on the standard and uncontested procedure section. So, first you will need to read chapter 8 to get a basic understanding of the forms and procedures, then read chapter 9 for additional instructions on handling the contested situation. Be sure to read through both chapters before you start filling out any forms.

6 General Procedures

An Introduction to Legal Forms

Many of the forms in this book follow forms created by the North Carolina Administrative Office of the Courts. All forms in this book are legally correct, however, one occasionally encounters a troublesome clerk or judge who is very particular about how he or she wants the forms. If you encounter any problem with the forms in this book being accepted by the clerk or judge, you can try one or more of the following:

- Ask the clerk or judge what is wrong with your form, then try to change it to suit the clerk or judge.
- Consult a lawyer.

Although the instructions in this book will tell you to "type in" certain information, it is not absolutely necessary to use a typewriter. If typing is not possible, you can print the information required in the forms. Just be sure to use black ink and that your handwriting can be easily read, or the clerk may not accept your papers for filing.

Each form is referred to by both the title of the form and a form number. Be sure to check the form number because some of the forms have similar titles. The form number is found in the top outside corner of the first page of each form. Also, a list of the forms, by both number and name, is found at the beginning of appendix B.

You will notice that most of the forms in appendix B of this book have the same heading. The forms without this heading are not filed with the court, but are for your use only. The top portion of these court forms will all be completed in the same manner. The heading at the very top of the form tells which court your case is filed in. You will need to type in the county in which the court is located.

Next, you need to type your full name and your spouse's full name, on the lines at the left side of the form, above the appropriate line depending upon whether you are the plaintiff or the defendant. The plaintiff is the person who is initiating the procedure. Do not use nicknames or shortened version of names. You should use the names as they appear on your marriage license, if possible. You won't be able to type in a "File Number" until after you file your Complaint with the clerk. The clerk will assign a case number and will write it on your Complaint and any other papers you file with it. You must type in the file number on all papers you file later.

When completed, the top portion of your forms should look something like the following example:

NORTH CAROLINA	)	IN THE GENERAL COURT OF JUSTICE
	)	
GUILFORD COUNTY	)	DISTRICT COURT DIVISION
	)	FILE NO:_______________
	)	
FRED FLINTSTONE ,	)	
Plaintiff,	)	
	)	DIVORCE COMPLAINT
	)	
WILMA FLINTSTONE	)	
Defendant.	)	

Filing With the Court Clerk

Once you have decided which forms you need, and have them all prepared, it is time to file your case with the court clerk. First, make at least three copies of each form (the original for the clerk, one copy for yourself, one for your spouse, and one extra just in case the clerk asks for two copies or you decide to hire an attorney later).

Filing is actually about as simple as making a bank deposit, although the following information will help things go smoothly. Call the court clerk's office. You can find the phone number under the county government section in your phone directory. Ask the clerk the following questions (along with any other questions that come to mind, such as where the clerk's office is located and their hours of operation):

- How much is the filing fee for a divorce?
- Does the court have any special forms that need to be filed with the complaint: (If there are special forms that do not appear in this book, you will need to go down to the clerk's office and pick them up. There may be a fee, so ask.)
- How many copies of the complaint and other forms do you need to file with the clerk?

Next, take your Complaint, and any other forms you determine you need, to the clerk's office. The clerk handles many different types of cases, so be sure to look for signs telling you which office or window to go to. You should be looking for signs that say such things as "District Court," "Civil Division," "Filing," etc. If it's too confusing, ask someone where you file a divorce complaint.

Once you've found the right place, simply hand the papers to the clerk and say, "I'd like to file this." The clerk will examine the papers, then do one of two things: either accept it for filing (and either collect the filing fee or direct you to where to pay it), or tell you that something is not correct. If you're told something is wrong, ask the clerk to explain to you what is wrong and how to correct the problem. Although clerks are not permitted to give legal advice, the types of problems they spot are usually very minor things that they can tell you how to correct.

Notifying Your Spouse

In each of the procedures described earlier you will be required to notify your spouse that you have filed for divorce. This gives your spouse a chance to respond to your Divorce Complaint. If you are unable to find your spouse, you will also need to read chapter 12.

Notice of Filing Complaint

The most common way to notify your spouse that you filed for a divorce is called *personal service*, which is where the sheriff, or an authorized process server, personally delivers the papers to your spouse.

Call the county sheriff's office in the county where your spouse lives, and ask how much it will cost to have him or her served with the divorce papers. It will probably cost about $5.00. Deliver, or mail, one copy of your Divorce Complaint (together with any other documents you filed), two copies including the original white copy of the Summons (Form 6), and a check or money order for the service fee, to the sheriff's office. You can obtain additional copies of the Summons from the Clerk's office.

To complete the Summons (Form 6) you need to:

1. In the upper left hand corner, fill in the name of the county where you will be filing the complaint.
2. Check the box labeled "District Court Division" in right hand corner of the form.
3. Fill in your name (you are the Plaintiff) and address as indicated.
4. Fill in the name of your spouse in the box labeled "Defendant."

5. In the box labeled "To" fill in the Sheriff Department if they will be serving the DIVORCE COMPLAINT. Write the name of the Defendant if you will be mailing the complaint certified mail.

6. Type the name and address of the Defendant in the box as indicated.

7. Type your address in the box as indicated.

8. Go to the clerk's office, and have the clerk sign the SUMMONS and file it along with the complaint.

A sheriff's deputy will personally deliver the papers to your spouse. Of course, you must give the sheriff accurate information about where your spouse can be found. If there are several addresses where your spouse might be found (such as home, a relative's, and work), enclose a letter to the sheriff with all of the addresses and any other information that may help the sheriff find your spouse (such as the hours your spouse works). The deputy will fill out the return of service on the back of the SUMMONS to verify that the papers were delivered (including the date and time they were delivered), and will file a copy with the court clerk.

CERTIFIED MAIL

Your spouse can also be served by *certified mail.* This method of service is often used when your spouse lives in another state. Also, if your spouse is a member of the armed services and you know their mailing address this is the most effective means of serving them. You need to send your spouse a copy of the complaint and other related documents and a copy of the SUMMONS. Do not send the original white copy of the SUMMONS.

If you use this method of service you will need to file an AFFIDAVIT OF SERVICE and attach a copy of the green card with your spouse's signature and the date it was received.

To complete the AFFIDAVIT OF SERVICE BY REGISTERED OR CERTIFIED MAIL (Form 11) you need to:

1. Fill in the top portion according to the instructions on page 62.
2. Fill in your name beside "Plaintiff" in the blank space in paragraph 1.
3. Fill in your spouses name beside the word Defendant in second paragraph.
4. Fill your spouses name and their address in line 2.
5. Fill in the date your spouse received the complaint on line 3.
6. Date and sign the form in the presence of a notary public.
7. Attach the green return receipt card to the affidavit.
8. File the AFFIDAVIT OF SERVICE BY REGISTERED OR CERTIFIED MAIL and the attached green card at the clerk's office.

You will also need to complete the Return of Service form on the back of the original white SUMMONS and file it with the clerk along with the AFFIDAVIT OF SERVICE BY REGISTERED OR CERTIFIED MAIL. First, check the box labeled "Other manner of service." Then write the following statement in the space provided:

Service was received on ______________ (*fill in the date*) and completed by certified mail.

The green card is attached to the AFFIDAVIT OF SERVICE BY REGISTERED OR CERTIFIED MAIL.

OTHER NOTICES

Once your spouse has been served with the DIVORCE COMPLAINT, you may simply mail him or her copies of any papers you file later. All you need to do is complete a form (called a *certificate of service*) stating that you mailed copies to your spouse. Some of the forms in this book will have a certificate of service for you to complete. If any form you filed does not contain one, you will need to complete the CERTIFICATE OF SERVICE (Form 8), in appendix B of this book. To complete the CERTIFICATE OF SERVICE (Form 8):

1. Complete the top portion according to the instructions on page 62.

2. Type in your name in the space provided on the first line of the text.
3. Type in the name of the document you are sending to your spouse in the space provided on the second line of the text.
4. Type in the name and address of the person to whom the papers are being sent (your spouse or your spouse's attorney).
5. Sign your name and file it with the clerk of court as proof that you sent a copy.

Once you get a hearing date set with the judge, you'll need to notify your spouse of the hearing by preparing a NOTICE OF HEARING (Form 7). Just fill in the top of the form according to the instructions in chapter 6, and fill in all of the blanks on the form for the day of the week, date, month, year, time, and location of the hearing. Then make three copies of the NOTICE OF HEARING, and mail one copy to your spouse. File the original with the court clerk and keep two copies for yourself.

SETTING A COURT HEARING

You will need to set a hearing date for the divorce hearing, or for any matters that require a hearing (these will be discussed later in this book). The court clerk will be able to give you a date. Ask the clerk for the location of the hearing. You'll need the courtroom number as well as the location within the building.

COURTROOM MANNERS

There are certain rules of procedure that are used in a court. These are really the rules of good conduct, or good manners, and are designed to keep things orderly. Many of the rules are written down, although some are unwritten customs that have just developed over many years. They aren't difficult, and most of them do make sense. Following these suggestions will make the judge respect you for your maturity and professional manner, and possibly even make him forget for a moment that you are not a lawyer. It will also increase the likelihood that you will get the things you request.

Show respect for the judge. This basically means, don't do anything to make the judge angry at you, such as arguing with him. Be polite, and call the judge "Your Honor" when you speak to him, such as "Yes, Your Honor," or "Your Honor, I brought proof of my income." Although many lawyers address judges as "Judge," this is not proper. Many of the following rules also relate to showing respect for the court. This also means wearing appropriate clothing, such as a coat and tie for men and a dress for women. This especially means no T-shirts, blue jeans, shorts, or "revealing" clothing.

Whenever the judge talks, you listen. Even if the judge interrupts you, stop talking immediately and listen. Judges tend to get angry when someone doesn't let them interrupt.

Only one person can talk at a time. Each person is allotted his or her own time to talk in court. The judge can only listen to one person at a time, so don't interrupt your spouse when it's his or her turn. And as difficult as it may be, stop talking if your spouse interrupts you. (Let the judge tell your spouse to keep quiet and let you have your say.)

Talk to the judge, not to your spouse. Many people get in front of a judge and begin arguing with each other. They actually turn away from the judge, face each other, and begin arguing as if they are in the room alone. This generally has several negative results: The judge can't understand what either one is saying since they both start talking at once, they both look like fools for losing control, and the judge gets angry with both of them. So whenever you speak in a courtroom, look only at the judge. Try to pretend that your spouse isn't there. Remember, you are there to convince the judge that you should have certain things. You don't need to convince your spouse.

Talk only when it's your turn. The usual procedure is for you to present your case first. When you are done saying all you came to say, your spouse will have a chance to say whatever he or she came to say. Let your spouse have his or her say. When he or she is finished you will get another chance to respond to what has been said.

Stick to the subject. Many people can't resist the temptation to get off the track and start telling the judge all the problems with their marriage over the past twenty years. This just wastes time, and aggravates the judge. So stick to the subject, and answer the judge's questions simply and to the point.

Keep calm. Judges like things to go smoothly in their courtrooms. They don't like shouting, name calling, crying, or other displays of emotion. Generally, judges don't like family law cases because they get too emotionally charged. So give your judge a pleasant surprise by keeping calm and focusing on the issues.

Show respect for your spouse. Even if you don't respect your spouse, act like you do. All you have to do is refer to your spouse as "Mr. Smith" or "Ms. Smith" (using his or her correct name, of course).

NEGOTIATING

It is beyond the scope and ability of this book to fully present a course in negotiation techniques. However, a few basic rules may be of some help.

Ask for more than you want. This always gives you some room to compromise by giving up a few things, and end up with close to what you really want. With property division, this means you will review your PROPERTY INVENTORY (Form 1), and decide which items you really want, would like to have, and don't care much about. Also try to figure out which items your spouse really wants, would like to have, and doesn't care much about. At the beginning you will say that you want certain things. Your list will include: (a) Everything you really want, (b) almost everything you'd like to have, (c) some of the things you don't care about, and (d) some of the things you think your spouse really wants or would like to have. Once you find out what is on your spouse's list, you begin trading items. Generally you try to give your spouse things that he really wants and that you don't care about, in return for your spouse giving you the items you really care about and would like to have.

Generally, child custody tends to be something that cannot be negotiated. It is more often used as a threat by one of the parties in order to get something else, such as more of the property, or lower child support. If the real issue is one of these other matters, don't be concerned by a threat of a custody fight. In these cases, the other party probably does not really want custody, and won't fight for it. If the real issue is custody, you won't be able to negotiate for it and will end up letting the judge decide anyway.

If you will be receiving child support, then you should first work out what you think the judge will order based upon the child support guidelines discussed in chapter 5. Then you should ask for more, and negotiate down to what the guidelines call for. If your spouse won't settle for something very close to the guidelines, give up trying to work it out and let the judge decide.

Let your spouse start the bidding. The first person to mention a dollar figure loses. Whether it's a child support figure or the value of a piece of property, try to get your spouse to name the amount he or she thinks it should be first. If your spouse starts with a figure close to what you had in mind, it will be much easier to get to your figure. If your spouse begins with a figure far from yours, you know how far in the other direction to begin your bid.

Give your spouse time to think and worry. Your spouse is probably just as afraid as you about the possibility of losing to the judge's decision, and would like to settle. Don't be afraid to state your "final offer," then walk away. Give your spouse a day or two to think it over. Maybe he or she will call back and make a better offer. If not, you can always "reconsider" and make a different offer in a few days, but don't be too willing to do this or your spouse may think you will give in even more.

Know your bottom line. Before you begin negotiating you should try to set a point that you will not go beyond. If you have decided that there are four items of property that you absolutely must have, and your spouse is only willing to agree to let you have three, it's time to end the bargaining session and go home.

Remember what you've learned. By the time you've read this far you should be aware of two things:

1. The judge will roughly divide your property equally.
2. The judge will probably come close to the child support guidelines.

This awareness should give you an approximate idea of how things will turn out if the judge is asked to decide these issues, which should help you to set your bottom line on them.

7 Standard Divorce Procedure

Can You Use the Standard Procedure?

In certain situations you may take advantage of what was previously referred to as the Standard Divorce Procedure. If you and your spouse have no assets, no minor children, and there are no alimony claims, then you should have no problem getting a divorce. If you don't meet all of these conditions, you may still want to read this section, as it will help you understand the other procedures better.

Basically, the standard divorce procedure is as follows:

1. Complete the necessary forms: complaint, verification, and summons.
2. File the appropriate forms with the clerk of court.
3. Serve the papers on your spouse.
4. Contact the clerk about a hearing date.
5. Notify your spouse about the hearing date.
6. Appear for a brief hearing with the judge.

The following is a discussion of the four possible forms used in the standard procedure, and of the procedure itself. You will definitely need to use all of these forms, and may need one or more of the others in the appendix depending upon your situation.

Divorce Complaint and Motion for Summary Judgment

This is simply the paper used to open your case and ask the judge for a divorce. To complete the Divorce Complaint and Motion for Summary Judgment (Form 9) you need to:

1. Complete the top portion according to the instructions on page 62.
2. Type in the name of the county you live in paragraph 1.
3. Type in the name of the county and state where your spouse lives, on the appropriate line in paragraph 2.
4. Type in the date you were married and state where you were married, on the appropriate line in paragraph 3.
5. Type in the date you were separated on line 4.
6. Indicate on line 7 whether or not you wish to resume the use of your maiden name. If you do, indicate the name you wish to resume on the appropriate line.
7. Type in your spouse's name on line 1 of the last page.
8. If you wish to resume the use of your maiden name, indicate the name you wish to resume on line 2 of the last page.
9. On the last page of the form, sign your name and fill in the date. Then, type in your address and phone number where indicated below the signature lines.

Verification

The VERIFICATION (Form 10) is filed as your affirmation that the information you included in the DIVORCE COMPLAINT AND MOTION FOR SUMMARY JUDGMENT (Form 9) regarding your residency, the date you were married and separated is true. Complete the top portion by filling in the name of the county and the file number. Then, you will need to sign and date the form in the presence of a notary public. After you've completed the form, it should be attached to the back of the DIVORCE COMPLAINT AND MOTION FOR SUMMARY JUDGMENT (Form 9).

Summary Judgment for Absolute Divorce

The SUMMARY JUDGMENT FOR ABSOLUTE DIVORCE (Form 12) is the paper the judge will sign at the divorce hearing to formally grant your divorce. To complete the SUMMARY JUDGMENT FOR ABSOLUTE DIVORCE (Form 12) you will need to:

1. Complete the top portion according to the instructions on page 62.
2. In the appropriate space in paragraph 1 fill in whether it was the Plaintiff (you) or the Defendant (your spouse) that has resided in North Carolina for at least six months prior to the filing for divorce.
3. Fill in when and where you were married and the date you separated in paragraph 2.
4. Indicate in paragraph 5 the name you wish to resume. If this does not apply to your situation, you can white out this paragraph.

The judge will fill in the date and sign the form at the final hearing.

Certificate of Absolute Divorce or Annulment

The Certificate of Absolute Divorce or Annulment (Form 13) is required by the courts for their own administrative purposes. To complete the Certificate of Absolute Divorce or Annulment (Form 13) you need to:

1. Fill in the file number and name of the county where the complaint was filed in the left hand corner.
2. On line 1 check the box that corresponds with whether or not you are the husband or wife and then type in your full name.
3. On line 2a fill in the name of the state where you live.
4. On line 2b fill in the name of the county where you live.
5. On line 3 indicate whether your spouse is the husband or wife and then type in their full name.
6. On line 4a fill in the name of the state where your spouse lives.
7. On line 4b fill in the name of the county where your spouse lives.
8. On line 5 indicate the date you were married.
9. On line 6 indicate the city and state where you were married.
10. On line 7 indicate the number of children you and your spouse had together.
11. On line 8 indicate the date you separated.

Do not write anything below the line identified as "Certification." The Clerk will fill in that information. (**Note:** You can obtain a copy of this form from the Clerk's office.)

8 Uncontested Divorce Procedure

This chapter will provide a general overview of the uncontested divorce procedure. The following chapters will discuss some of these procedures in more detail.

Contested or Uncontested Divorce?

Most lawyers have had the following experience: A new client comes in, saying she wants to file for divorce. She has discussed it with her husband, and it will be a "simple, uncontested" divorce. Once the papers are filed the husband and wife begin arguing over a few items of property. The lawyer then spends a lot of time negotiating with the husband. After much arguing, an agreement is finally reached. The case will proceed in the court as "uncontested," but only after a lot of "contesting" out of court.

For purposes of this book, a *contested* case is one where you and your spouse will be doing your arguing in court, and leaving the decision to the judge. An *uncontested* case is one where you will do your arguing and deciding before court, and the judge will only be approving your decision.

You probably won't know if you are going to have a contested case until you try the uncontested route and fail. Therefore, the following sections are presented mostly to assist you in attempting the uncontested case. Chapter 9 specifically discusses the contested case.

There are actually two ways that a case can be considered uncontested. One is where you and your spouse reach an agreement on every issue in the divorce. To be in this situation you must be in an agreement on the following points:

1. How your property is to be divided.
2. How your debts are to be divided.
3. Which of you will have custody of the children.
4. How much child support is to be paid by the person not having custody.
5. Whether any alimony is to be paid, and if so, how much and for how long a period of time.

In situations where you have minor children, major assets or debts and desire alimony, and you and your spouse are able to resolve these matters, the divorce is still a simple procedure.

Once you and your spouse decide on the terms, you prepare a separation agreement that outlines exactly who is going to get what and who is going to do what. You both sign it in the presence of a notary and make three copies; one for your spouse, one to attach to the DIVORCE JUDGMENT, and two to keep for your personal records. Only the party who filed the action needs to attend the hearing.

The other type of uncontested case is where your spouse simply does not respond to the petition. If you have your spouse served by the sheriff or certified mail (as described in chapter 6), and he or she does not respond, you will need to appear in court and have a hearing. Alimony, custody, and equitable distribution are not decided by default. However, if your spouse does not appear at the hearing (you still must send NOTICE OF HEARING even if your spouse doesn't respond to the DIVORCE COMPLAINT) the judge will grant the relief you request since their is no one to rebut your testimony. You should be prepared and take whatever you need to tell your side of the story and to support whatever it is you are asking the judge to do.

To begin your divorce case, the following forms should be filed with the court clerk in all cases (see chapter 6, for filing instructions):

1. DIVORCE COMPLAINT (Form 14)
2. VERIFICATION (Form 10)
3. SUMMONS (Form 6)

Other forms which you determine to be necessary will also be filed, either with your petition or at any time before the final hearing, depending upon your situation. The following forms will be prepared in advance, but will not be filed until the final hearing:

1. DIVORCE JUDGMENT (Form 20)
2. CERTIFICATE OF ABSOLUTE DIVORCE OR ANNULMENT (Form 13)
3. SEPARATION AGREEMENT (Form 16 or 17)

Once all of the necessary forms have been filed and your spouse is served, you will need to contact the clerk to arrange a hearing date for the divorce hearing (see the section on Setting a Court Hearing in chapter 6). You should tell the clerk that you need to schedule a "final hearing for an uncontested divorce."

The following sections give instructions for when you need each form, and how to complete it.

DIVORCE COMPLAINT

The DIVORCE COMPLAINT (Form 14) is simply the paper you file with the court to begin your case and to ask the judge to give you a divorce.

To complete your DIVORCE COMPLAINT (Form 14), you need to:

1. Complete the top portion according to the instructions on page 62.
2. Fill in the county where the complaint will be filed and where you live on line 1.
3. Fill in the name of the county and state where the Defendant lives on line 2.
4. Fill in the date and place of your marriage on line 3.
5. Fill in the date you were separated on line 4.
6. Fill in the number, name, and birthdates of your minor children on line 5.
7. Indicate on line 6 whether or not you and your spouse have resolved issues of child support, custody, alimony, or equitable distribution, or which of these matters needs to be resolved at a later time.
8. Fill in the name of your spouse on line 1 of the second section of the form.
9. Check the box that applies to your situation in line 2.
10. On the last page, type in the date, sign your name, and write in your address and telephone number below the signature line.
11. Complete a VERIFICATION (Form 10) according to the instruction in chapter 7 and attach it to the DIVORCE COMPLAINT.

Your complaint is now ready for filing. Be sure to prepare the SUMMONS (Form 6) to go along with the DIVORCE COMPLAINT. (See chapter 6.)

SEPARATION AND PROPERTY SETTLEMENT AGREEMENT

The SEPARATION AND PROPERTY SETTLEMENT AGREEMENT (Form 16) is not a form created by the Bar Association or the Administrative Office of the Courts. It is intended to provide you with a variety of standard provisions often used in these type of agreements. For example, this form includes provisions for agreements on child support and custody, alimony, and property agreements. Whether you and your spouse agreed on everything from the start, or whether you've gone through extensive negotiations to reach an agreement, you need to put your agreement in writing. This is done through a separation agreement. Even if you don't agree on everything, you should put what you do agree on into a written agreement.

To complete the SEPARATION AND PROPERTY SETTLEMENT AGREEMENT (Form 16) you need to:

1. Fill in the name of county in the upper left hand corner.
2. Type in your name and your spouse's name in the blanks in the first paragraph; and type in the date you were married.
3. In each section there are boxes for you to check the provision that applies to your situation. Read through each one and look for places you need to mark a box or type in information to fit your situation.
4. You will type in the names of your children in the CHILD CUSTODY section. Physical custody refers to with whom each child will live. Any special arrangements you wish to include in this section can be typed in by the last box in this section.
5. The section on CHILD SUPPORT will require you to type in an amount and a period, such as "583.20" per "month." You will also

need to check the box for either "Husband" or "Wife" in the sections on child support and health insurance.

6. There are three possible boxes to check in the Alimony section. Check the first box if no alimony is to be paid by either you or your spouse. The second box is to be checked if you and your spouse have agreed to alimony. If so, you will also need to check the appropriate box for who is to pay the alimony, and fill in the amount, when that amount is to be paid (weekly, monthly, etc.), and for how long. The last box to check is if there are any special agreements regarding alimony.
7. Each of you should sign and date the form in the presence of a notary where indicated at the bottom of the form.

Separation Agreement

The Separation Agreement (Form 17) can be used as an alternative to the Separation and Property Settlement Agreement (Form 16). It can be used if you and your spouse own real property or would simply like to provide more details regarding the terms of your agreement. You can retype the form and exclude provisions that do not apply.

Note: If your agreement includes the transfer of real property you should consult a real property attorney about preparing the deed and recording the separation agreement with the register of deeds office.

Affidavit as to Status of Minor Child

The Affidavit as to Status of Minor Child (Form 18) may be required if you have minor children. You will need to complete a separate form for each of your minor children. To complete the Affidavit as to Status of Minor Child (Form 18) you need to:

1. Fill in the file number in the upper left hand corner.
2. Fill in the name of the county and your name and address and your spouse's name and address in the space provided in the upper left hand column.
3. Fill in your child's name, birthdate and place of birth in the space provided on the upper right hand side of the form.
4. In the middle section of the form, type in the period of residence and addresses where the child has lived for the past five years. If the child is not yet five years old, type in the places and period of residence since birth. You will also need to include the names and current addresses of persons with whom the child has lived during the past five years. You and your spouse should be referred to as "Plaintiff" and "Defendant."
5. Indicate by a check mark whether or not you have participated in litigation concerning the child in this or any other state, and whether there is someone other than you or your spouse who exercises visitation or custody rights with the child.
6. Take the form to a notary and date and sign the form in the box designated as "Signature of Affiant."

Acceptance of Service

You can simplify and speed up your case by having your spouse sign an ACCEPTANCE OF SERVICE (Form 19) before a notary public. If this form is used, you will not need to go through the procedure in chapter 6 on notifying your spouse.

To complete the ACCEPTANCE OF SERVICE (Form 19), you need to:

1. Complete the top portion according to the instructions on page 62.
2. Type in your spouse's name in the blank space in the first sentence.

3. Type in your name in the blank space in line 2.
4. Have your spouse sign on the "Signature" line before a notary public.

Note: You will still need to prepare a SUMMONS. Give your spouse a DIVORCE COMPLAINT with a yellow copy of the SUMMONS attached. Be sure to complete the Return of Service form on the back of the original white copy of the SUMMONS and file it with the clerk. To complete the Return of Service form check the box labeled "Other manner of service." Then write the following statement in the space provided:

The Defendant accepted service on ______________________.

DIVORCE JUDGMENT

The DIVORCE JUDGMENT (Form 20) will be completed in all divorce cases, except that some of the provisions will vary slightly depending on type of procedure used. If you and your spouse have agreed on the terms and entered into a separation agreement you should give your spouse a copy of the DIVORCE JUDGMENT before the hearing, to ensure he or she is aware of what it says, and agrees with it.

To complete the DIVORCE JUDGMENT (Form 20) you need to:

1. Complete the top portion according to the instructions on page 62.
2. Type in the date of the hearing, the name of the county, and city where the hearing will be held.
3. On line 1, fill in the date the DIVORCE COMPLAINT (Form 14) was filed.
4. Fill in the manner of service ("Sheriff," "Certified Mail," "Publication," or "Acceptance of Service") and the date your spouse (the Defendant) received the complaint on line 2.

5. Fill in the date you were married and separated on line 1 of the second section of the form.
6. Fill in the names and ages of your minor children on line 2 of the form.
7. Check the appropriate box(es) on line 4 of the second section of the form.
8. Fill in the state and county where both you and your spouse live on line 5 of the second section of the form.
9. Fill in your name and your spouse's name in the blanks provided in the first paragraph of the final section of the form.
10. Check the appropriate box(es) in the second section of the form.
11. The judge will date and sign the form.

If the judge tells you to change something major in the DIVORCE JUDGMENT, or if you had a contested hearing, it may not be possible to prepare it at the hearing. You will need to make a note of exactly what changes the judge requires, or what he or she ordered, then go home and prepare the DIVORCE JUDGMENT the way he or she instructed. You will then need to take the revised form back to the judge for his or her signature.

If you need to prepare the DIVORCE JUDGMENT after the hearing, you will also complete a CERTIFICATE OF SERVICE (Form 8), attach it to the DIVORCE JUDGMENT and deliver to the court clerk. Also give him or her two extra copies, along with a stamped envelope addressed to yourself and a stamped envelope addressed to your spouse. Ask the clerk whether you should sign and date the certificate of service. Sometimes the clerk will handle the mailing of the judgment after the judge signs it, in which case he or she may sign the CERTIFICATE OF SERVICE.

REQUEST BY SUPPORTING PARTY FOR WAGE WITHHOLDING

The REQUEST BY SUPPORTING PARTY FOR WAGE WITHHOLDING (Form 21) can be used in situations where your spouse agrees to have the child support obligation withheld from their paycheck. After your spouse completes this form, the Clerk will prepare an order to the employer of the person required to make the payment, requiring the employer to deduct the payment from the person's paycheck and send it to the clerk's office. This form should be prepared after the divorce hearing. It should be presented to the Clerk; not the Judge.

To complete the REQUEST BY SUPPORTING PARTY FOR WAGE WITHHOLDING (Form 21) :

1. Fill in the name of the county and file number on the top portion of the form.
2. Check the boxes designated as "District" and "Civil" on the top portion of the form.
3. Fill in your name beside the word "Plaintiff," and your spouse's name beside the word "Defendant."
4. Fill in the name, mailing and location address of the supporting party's employer in the box on the left hand side of the form.
5. Fill in the name, address and social security number of the supporting party in the boxes provided on the right hand side of the form.
6. In paragraph 1, fill in the requested information. In most instances the date of the support order will be the date your divorce judgment is signed.
7. In paragraph 2, fill in the amount of the supporting party's disposable wages. Disposable wages refers to their take-home pay.

8. Check the applicable boxes in paragraph 3, 4, and 5.
9. The supporting party should date and sign the bottom portion of the form.
10. The supporting party will also need to take the form to a notary and sign the verification on the back of the form.

9 Contested Divorce Procedure

Procedure Differences from Uncontested Divorce

This book cannot turn you into a trial lawyer. It can be very risky to try to handle a contested case yourself, although it has been done. There are several differences between a contested and an uncontested case. First, in an uncontested case the judge will usually go along with whatever you and your spouse have worked out. In a contested case you need to prove that you are entitled to what you are asking for. This means you will need a longer time for the hearing, you will need to present papers as evidence, and you may need to have witnesses testify for you.

Second, you may have to do some extra work to get the evidence you need, such as sending out subpoenas (which are discussed in the next section of this chapter), or even hiring a private investigator. Also, you will need to pay extra attention to assure that your spouse is properly notified of any court hearings, and that he or she is sent copies of any papers you file with the court clerk.

When it becomes apparent that you have a contested divorce, it is probably time to consider hiring an attorney, especially if the issue of child custody is involved. If you are truly ready to go to war over custody, it shows that this is an extremely important matter for you, and you may want to get professional assistance. You can predict a contested case when your spouse is seriously threatening to fight you every inch of the way, or when he or she hires an attorney.

On the other hand, you shouldn't assume that you need an attorney just because your spouse has hired one. Sometimes it will be easier to deal with the attorney than with your spouse. The attorney is not as emotionally involved and may see your settlement proposal as reasonable. So discuss things with your spouse's attorney first and see if things can be worked out. You can always hire your own lawyer if your spouse's isn't reasonable. Just be very cautious about signing any papers until you are certain you understand what they mean. You may want to have an attorney review any papers prepared by your spouse's lawyer before you sign them.

Aside from deciding if you want a lawyer, there are two main procedural differences between the uncontested and the contested divorce. First, you will need to be more prepared for the hearing. Second, you will not prepare the DIVORCE JUDGMENT (Form 20) until after the hearing with the judge. This is because you won't know what to put in the DIVORCE JUDGMENT until the judge decides the various matters in dispute.

The next chapters will discuss how to prepare for the issues to be argued at the hearing, and how to prepare the DIVORCE JUDGMENT.

COLLECTING INFORMATION

The judge will require a FINANCIAL AFFIDAVIT (Form 15) from you, and also one from your spouse. If your spouse has indicated that he or she will not cooperate at all, and will not provide a FINANCIAL AFFIDAVIT, you may have to try to get the information yourself. You can go to the hearing and tell the judge that your spouse won't cooperate, but the judge may just issue an order requiring your spouse to provide information (or be held in contempt of court), and continue the hearing to another date. It may help to speed things up if you are able to get the information yourself, and have it available at the hearing. This will require you to get subpoenas issued.

Before you send a SUBPOENA to your spouse's employer, bank, or accountant, you need to let your spouse know what you are about to do. The thought that you are about to get these other people involved in your divorce may be enough to get your spouse to cooperate. If your spouse calls and says "I'll give you the information," give him or her a few days to follow through. Ask when you can expect to receive the FINANCIAL AFFIDAVIT, and offer to send your spouse another blank copy if he or she needs one. If your spouse sends a completed FINANCIAL AFFIDAVIT as promised, don't send the subpoena. If your spouse doesn't follow through, go ahead with the SUBPOENA. You can send out subpoenas to as many people or organizations as you need, but you'll need to use the following procedure for each SUBPOENA.

The SUBPOENA (Form 22). will eventually be sent to whomever you want to get information from or to appear at the hearing. Look at the FINANCIAL AFFIDAVIT form, and see what type of information is asked for. If you were able to do a good job making copies of important papers while preparing to file for divorce, you should have the information you need to figure out where you need to send subpoenas. Your spouse's income information can be obtained from his or her employer. Stock and bond information can be obtained from his or her stock broker, bank account balances from the bank, auto loan balances from the lender, etc. You can have subpoenas issued to any or all of these places, but don't overdo it. Concentrate on income information (especially if you are asking for child support or expect to pay child support), and information on the major property items. And, it may not be necessary to send out subpoenas if you already have recent copies of the papers relating to these items. You can always show the judge the copies of your spouse's paystubs, W-2 tax statements, or other papers at the hearing.

To complete the SUBPOENA (Form 22) you need to:

1. Complete the top portion according to the instructions on page 62.
2. Check the box to indicate whether or not you are the Plaintiff or Defendant.
3. Type your spouse's employer (or brokers, bankers, etc.) name and address after the word "TO:".
4. Check the appropriate box to indicate whether you want the person to appear as a witness or to produce documents. (Also include your spouse's social security number, or any information that will help the person receiving the subpoena to know what you are asking for.)
5. Indicate the location of the court, the date and time the person is to appear or produce documents.
6. Type in your name, address, and phone number.
7. Leave the date and clerk's signature spaces blank.

Next, have the sheriff personally serve the SUBPOENA to the person or place named in the SUBPOENA. The sheriff will need at least one extra copy of the SUBPOENA, and a check for the service fee. The employer, bank, etc., should send you the requested information. If the employer, bank, etc., calls you and says you must pay for copies, ask him how much they will cost and send a check or money order (if the amount isn't too high and you don't already have some fairly recent income information). If the employer, bank, etc., doesn't provide the information, you can try sending a letter to the employer, bank, etc., saying: "unless you provide the information requested in the SUBPOENA in seven days, a motion for contempt will be filed with the district court." This may scare the employer, bank, etc., into sending you the information. The sheriff will have also filed an affidavit verifying when the subpoena was served. There are more procedures you could go through to force the employer, bank, etc., to give the information, but it probably isn't worth the hassle and you'd probably need an attorney to help you with it. At the final hearing you can tell the judge that your spouse refused to provide income information, and that the SUBPOENA was not honored by the employer. The judge may do something to help you out, or he or she may advise you to see a lawyer.

There is also a procedure where you send written questions to your spouse, which he or she must answer in writing and under oath. These written questions are called *interrogatories*. If your spouse didn't file a FINANCIAL AFFIDAVIT, he or she probably won't answer the interrogatories either, which would leave you no better off. However, if you would like to try this, you may be able to locate sample interrogatories in a form book at the law library.

Once you collect the information needed, you can prepare for the hearing.

PROPERTY AND DEBTS

Generally, the judge will look at your property and debts, and will try to divide them "fairly." This does not necessarily mean they will be divided 50-50. What you want to do is offer the judge a reasonable solution that looks "fair." Adultery or other misconduct on the part of one party may not be used to justify an unequal division of property and debts.

It's time to review the PROPERTY INVENTORY (Form 1) and the DEBT INVENTORY (Form 2) you prepared earlier. For each item or property, note which of the following categories it fits into (it may fit into more than one):

1. You really want.
2. You'd like to have.
3. You don't care either way.

4. Your spouse really wants.
5. Your spouse would like to have.
6. Your spouse doesn't care either way.

Now start a list of what each of you should end up with, using the categories listed above. You will eventually end up with a list of things you can probably get with little difficulty (you really want and your spouse doesn't care), those which you'll fight over (you both really want), and those which need to be divided but can probably be easily divided equally (you both don't really care).

At the hearing, the judge will probably try to get you to work out your disagreements, but he or she won't put up with arguing for very long. In the end he or she will arbitrarily divide the items you can't agree upon, or order you to sell those items and divide the money you get equally.

On the few items that are really important to you it may be necessary for you to try to prove why you should get them. It will help if you can convince the judge of one or more of the following:

1. You paid for the item out of your own earnings or funds.
2. You are the one who primarily uses that item.
3. You use the item in your employment, business, or hobby.
4. You are willing to give up something else you really want in exchange for that item. (Of course you will try to give up something from your "don't care" or your "like to have" list.)
5. The item is needed for your children (assuming you will have custody).

The best thing you can do is make up a list of how you think the property should be divided. And make it a reasonably fair and equal list, regardless of how angry you are at your spouse. Even if the judge changes some of it to appear fair to your spouse, you will most likely get more of what you want than if you don't offer a suggestion. (No, this is not an exception to the negotiating rule of letting your spouse make the first offer, because at this point you are no longer just negotiating with your spouse. You are now negotiating with the judge. At this point you are trying to impress the judge with your fairness; not trying to convince your spouse.)

Special problems arise if a claim of separate property becomes an issue. This may be in terms of your spouse trying to get your separate property, or in terms of you trying to get property you feel your spouse is wrongly claiming to be separate. Basically, separate property is property either of you had before you were married, and kept separate. (If you need to review exactly what is marital and separate property, refer to page 40, and Section 50-20 of the General Statutes of North Carolina in appendix A.)

It is also a good idea to have any papers that prove that the property you claim to be nonmarital property is actually separate property. These would be papers showing that:

1. You bought the item before you were married (such as dated sales receipts);

2. You inherited the item as your own property (such as certified copies of wills and probate court papers); or

3. You got the property by exchanging it for property you had before you got married, or for property you received as a gift or through an inheritance (such as a statement from the person you made the exchange with, or some kind of receipt showing what was exchanged).

If you want to get at assets your spouse is claiming are separate assets, you will need to collect the following types of evidence:

- Papers showing that you helped pay for the asset (such as a check that you wrote, or bank statements showing that your money went into the same account that was used to make payments on the asset). For example, suppose your spouse purchased a house before you got married. During your marriage you made some of the mortgage payments with your own checking account (you will have cancelled checks, hopefully with the mortgage account number on them, to prove this). At other times, you deposited some of your paychecks into your spouse's checking account, and your spouse wrote checks from that account to pay the mortgage (again, there should be some bank records and cancelled checks that show that this was done). Since you contributed to the purchase of the house, you can claim some of the value of the house as a marital asset.

☛ Papers showing that you paid for repairs of the asset. If you paid for repairs on the home, or a car your spouse had before you were married, you can claim part of the value.

☛ Papers showing that the asset was improved, or increased in value during your marriage. Example 1: Your spouse owned the house before you were married. During your marriage you and your spouse added a family room to the house. This will enable you to make a claim for some of the value of the house. Example 2: Your spouse owned the house before you were married. The day before you got married, the house was worth $85,000. Now the house is appraised at $115,000. You can claim part of the $30,000 of increased value.

To make a claim on what would otherwise appear to be your spouse's separate property, you will need to request it. The form(s) you need to file are governed by local court rules. To successfully obtain separate property you'll need the assistance of an attorney in preparing forms.

At the hearing, the judge will have to look at whatever papers you show him, listen to what you and any witnesses say and then decide if you are entitled to any of the value of the property.

During the hearing the judge will announce who gets which items. Make a list of this as the judge tells you. Then, complete the DIVORCE JUDGMENT (Form 20) according to what the judge says. Once you have completed the DIVORCE JUDGMENT, make a copy and send it to your spouse. Send the original to the judge (not the court clerk), along with a completed CERTIFICATE OF SERVICE (Form 8) stapled to it showing the date you sent a copy to your spouse. If your spouse doesn't object to how you've prepared the Judgment, the judge will sign the judgment and return a copy to you. You should send the judge the original and two copies of the DIVORCE JUDGMENT, along with two stamped envelopes (one addressed to yourself, and the other addressed to your spouse).

CHILD CUSTODY AND VISITATION

Generally, if you are the wife, the odds start out in favor of you getting custody. But don't depend upon the odds. Start out by reviewing the guidelines the judge will use to decide the custody question. These can be found in chapter 5. For each item listed in that section, write down an explanation of how that item applies to you. This will be your argument when you have your hearing with the judge.

Many custody battles revolve around the moral fitness of one or both of the parents. If you become involved in this type of a custody fight, you should consult a lawyer. Charges of moral unfitness (such as illegal drug use, child abuse, immoral sexual conduct) can require long court hearings involving the testimony of many witnesses, as well as possibly the employment of private investigators. For such a hearing you will require the help of an attorney, who knows the law, what questions to ask witnesses, and the rules of evidence.

However, if the only question is whether you or your spouse have been the main caretaker of the child, you can always have friends, neighbors, and relatives come into the hearing (if they are willing to help you out) to testify on your behalf. And it may not be necessary for you to have an attorney. But, if you need to subpoena unwilling witnesses to testify, you should have an attorney.

The judge's decision regarding custody will have to be put into the DIVORCE JUDGMENT (Form 20). Read chapter 8 for instructions on preparing the DIVORCE JUDGMENT.

CHILD SUPPORT

In North Carolina, as in most states, child support is mostly a matter of a mathematical calculation. Getting a fair child support amount depends upon the accuracy of the income information presented to the judge. If you feel fairly sure that the information your spouse presents is accurate, or that you have obtained accurate information about his or her income, there isn't much to argue about. The judge will simply take the income information provided, use the formula to calculate the amount to be paid, and order that amount to be paid.

In most cases, there won't be much room to argue about the amount of child support, so there usually isn't a need to get an attorney. If you claim your spouse has not provided accurate income information, it will be up to you to prove this to the judge by showing the income information you have obtained from your spouse's employer or other source of income.

The only areas open for argument are whatever special needs are claimed by the party asking for child support. Once again, it will be necessary for that party to provide proof of the cost of these special needs by producing billing statements, receipts, or other papers to show the amount of these needs.

The judge's decision regarding child support will have to be put into the DIVORCE JUDGMENT (Form 20). Read chapter 8 for instructions on preparing the DIVORCE JUDGMENT.

ALIMONY

A dispute over alimony may require a lawyer, especially if there is a request for permanent alimony because of a disability. Such a claim may require the testimony of expert witnesses (such as doctors, accountants, and actuaries), which requires the special knowledge of an attorney. A charge of adultery may also require a lawyer and possibly a private investigator as well.

If alimony has been requested, take a look at the DIVORCE COMPLAINT (Form 14), or other court paper asking for alimony, and review the reasons alimony was requested. These reasons will be the subject of the court hearing on this question. You should determine what information (including papers and the testimony of witnesses) you will need to present to the judge to either support or refute the reasons alimony was requested.

For postseparation support or temporary alimony, the most common reason is that the person needs help until he or she can get training to enter the work force. The questions that will need to be answered are:

1. What has the person been trained for in the past?
2. What type of training is needed before the person can again be employable in that field?
3. How long will this training take?
4. What amount of income can be expected upon employment?
5. How much money is required for the training?

Questions that may be asked in either a temporary or a permanent alimony situation include an examination of the situation of the parties during their marriage that led to the person not working, what contribution to the marriage that person made, and what other factors exist that makes an award of alimony appropriate. You should be prepared to present evidence regarding these questions.

The Court Hearing 10

Preparation

Hearing Dates

See chapter 6 for instructions on how to set a hearing date.

Notifying Your Spouse

Now that you've got a hearing date set with the judge, you'll need to notify your spouse when the hearing will be. Just fill in the NOTICE OF HEARING (Form 7) according to the instructions in chapter 6. Then make three copies of the NOTICE OF HEARING. File the original with the court clerk, mail one copy to your spouse and keep two copies for yourself.

What Papers to Bring

Bring your copies (if available) of the following papers to the hearing:

- Your DIVORCE COMPLAINT (Form 14) and the affidavits you attached to it.
- Any papers you may have showing that your spouse was properly notified of the divorce (although the original summons with the Sheriff's certification will be in the court file, and you may not have a copy).
- SEPARATION AND PROPERTY SETTLEMENT AGREEMENT (Form 16) or SEPARATION AGREEMENT (Form 17).
- DIVORCE JUDGMENT (Form 20).
- CERTIFICATE OF ABSOLUTE DIVORCE OR ANNULMENT (Form 13).

The Hearing

The hearing will probably take place in a large courtroom like you see on TV or in the movies. Although it is not likely to be as lavish. Generally, the room will be filled with other people seeking the same thing you are.

The hearing will start once you are sworn in. The judge will then review the file to ensure your paperwork is in order and that your spouse was properly served and notified of the divorce hearing. The judge may then ask how long you have lived in the state, how long you have been separated and if there are any issues of alimony, equitable distribution or custody pending between you and your spouse. If it applies the judge might also ask if you would like to resume the use of your maiden name. The judge will then review your divorce judgment and divorce certificate.

If you have any information that is different and more current than what is in the Financial Affidavits, you should mention to the judge that you have more current information. You will then give a copy of whatever papers you have to show the changed situation (such as current paystub showing an increase in pay, or a current bank statement showing a new balance). The judge may ask to see any papers you have to prove what you've put in your Financial Affidavit. Your basic job at the hearing is to answer the judge's questions, and give the judge the information he or she needs to give you a divorce.

If there are any items that you and your spouse have not yet agreed upon, tell the judge what these items are. Refer to chapter 9, relating to the contested divorce, for more information about how to handle these unresolved issues. Be prepared to make a suggestion as to how these matters should be settled, and to explain to the judge why your suggestion is the best solution.

If the judge asks for any information that you haven't brought with you, tell the judge that you don't have it with you but you will be happy to provide him or her with the information by the end of the following day. Just be sure you get the papers to the judge!

At the end of the hearing the judge will tell you if he or she is going to grant you a divorce and accept your settlement agreement. It would be very unusual for the judge not to grant the divorce and accept your agreement. You will then tell the judge that you have prepared a proposed judgment, and hand the judge the original. Refer to chapter 8 regarding how to prepare the DIVORCE JUDGMENT (Form 20). You should have two extra copies of the Judgment with you, one for yourself and one for your spouse. You should also bring two envelopes, one addressed to yourself and one addressed to your spouse, and two stamps. This is in case the judge wants to review the DIVORCE JUDGMENT and mail it to you later, instead of signing it at the hearing. If the judge wants you to make any changes in the DIVORCE JUDGMENT, make a careful note of exactly what the judge wants (ask him or her to explain it again if you didn't understand the first time), then tell the judge that you will make the correction and deliver the judgment the following day. If the change requested is a small one, you might even be able to write in the change by hand at the hearing.

When the hearing is over, thank the judge and leave. The judge will sign the original DIVORCE JUDGMENT, and send it to the court clerk's office to be entered in the court's file.

If any serious problems develop at the hearing (such as your spouse's attorney starts making a lot of technical objections, or the judge gives you a hard time), just tell the judge you'd like to continue the hearing so you can retain an attorney. Then go get one!

Child Support Agencies

There are two agencies you need to be aware of:

Central Depository

The Central Depository is the agency that processes the child support and alimony payments. This is frequently a division of the court clerk's office. The spouse responsible to pay the support (or his or her employer) will make payments to the depository. The depository then cashes that check and issues a check to the spouse entitled to receive support or alimony. Sometimes the judge's secretary or the court clerk will take an extra copy of the Divorce Judgment and send it to the Central Depository. The Central Depository keeps the official records of what has and has not been paid.

Child Support Enforcement Office

The Child Support Enforcement office is responsible for enforcing the payment of child support to parents receiving welfare (Aid to Families with Dependent Children), and others who request their services. If you are to receive support and you would like to use the enforcement services of this office, you will need to contact your local Child Support Enforcement Office. This may not be necessary if your spouse goes on a wage withholding order immediately, and keeps his or her job. But if some payments are missed, you may call the Child Support Enforcement Office at any time and ask for their assistance.

11 When You Can't Find Your Spouse

Your spouse has run off, and you have no idea of where he or she might be. So how do you have the sheriff deliver a copy of your DIVORCE COMPLAINT (Form 14) to your spouse? The answer is, you can't use the sheriff. Instead of personal service you will use a method of giving notice called *service by publication*. This is one of the most complicated procedures in the legal system. You will need to follow the steps listed below very carefully.

The Diligent Search

The court will only permit publication when you can't locate your spouse. This also includes the situation where the sheriff has tried several times to personally serve your spouse, but it appears that your spouse is hiding to avoid being served. First, you'll have to show that you can't locate your spouse by letting the court know what you've done to try to find him or her. In making this search you should try the following:

- Check the phone book and directory assistance in the area where you live.
- Check directory assistance in the area where you last knew your spouse to be.

- Ask friends and relatives who might know where your spouse might be.
- Check with the post office where he or she last lived to see if there is a forwarding address. (You can ask by mail if it is too far away.)
- Check records of the tax collector and property assessor to see if your spouse owns property.
- Write to the Department of Motor Vehicles to see if your spouse has any car registrations.
- Check with any other sources you know that may lead you to a current address (such as landlords, prior employers, etc.).
- If your spouse is a member of the military, your local Child Support Enforcement Agency may be able to assist you in locating them if you know their social security number and their branch of service.

If you do come up with a current address, go back to personal service by the sheriff or certified mail, but if not, continue with this procedure.

Preparing and Filing Court Papers

Once you have made your search you need to prepare a Notice of Service by Publication (Form 23). This form spells out what you need the newspaper to publish.

To complete the Notice of Service by Publication (Form 23) you need to:

1. Type the name of the name of the county in the space provided in the heading.
2. Type in the last date in which your spouse needs to respond. (It must be at least forty days after the date of the first publication of the notice or the date the complaint was required to be filed whichever is later.)

3. Date and sign the notice. You should also include your address or telephone number.

You will also need to prepare an AFFIDAVIT OF PUBLICATION (Form 24). This form will be filled in by someone so authorized at the newspaper. It verifies that the notice was actually published in the newspaper. They are required to attach a copy of the notice as it appeared in the newspaper to the AFFIDAVIT OF PUBLICATION. The person at the newspaper who fills out the form will know how to complete it. This completed form should be attached to the AFFIDAVIT OF SERVICE BY PUBLICATION (Form 25).

PUBLISHING

Your next step is to have a newspaper publish your NOTICE OF SERVICE BY PUBLICATION (Form 23). Check the Yellow Pages listings under "Newspapers," and call several of the smaller ones in your county (making sure it is in the same area as where you believe your spouse is located or if you have no idea about their whereabouts, then in the same county as the court). Ask if they are approved for legal announcements. If they are, ask how much they charge to publish a NOTICE OF SERVICE BY PUBLICATION. What you are searching for is the cheapest paper. Most areas have a paper that specializes in the publishing of legal announcements, at a much cheaper rate than the regular daily newspapers. If you look around the courthouse you may be able to find a copy or newsstand for this paper.

Once you've found the paper you want, send them a copy of the NOTICE OF SERVICE BY PUBLICATION (Form 23), along with the AFFIDAVIT OF PUBLICATION (Form 24).

After the notice has been published and prior to the divorce hearing, you will need to complete an AFFIDAVIT OF SERVICE BY PUBLICATION (Form 25).

To complete the AFFIDAVIT OF SERVICE BY PUBLICATION (Form 25) you need to:

1. Complete the top portion according to the instructions in chapter 6.
2. Fill in your name on the blank space on the first line.
3. File in the name of the newspaper on line 4.
4. Check the appropriate box on line 5. If applicable, fill in your spouse's last known address.
5. Explain why your spouse could not be served by the sheriff or certified mail.
6. Check the appropriate box in line 7. If applicable, explain why you selected the area you chose to publish the notice.
7. Take the form to a notary public and sign the form.
8. Attach the AFFIDAVIT OF PUBLICATION (Form 24) and file in the clerk's office.

The NOTICE OF SERVICE BY PUBLICATION (Form 23) will be published once a week for three successive weeks. Get a copy of the paper the first time it will appear and check to be sure it was printed correctly. If you find an error, notify the newspaper immediately.

Look at the date that your spouse has to respond. You must make sure that this date is at least forty days after the date the newspaper first published the notice or the date the complaint was filed, whichever is later. If these requirements are not met, notify the newspaper of *their* mistake. You will also need to prepare a new notice and go through the procedure again. If the newspaper made the mistake, they should not charge you for the second publication.

As indicated in the NOTICE OF SERVICE BY PUBLICATION, your spouse has until a certain date to respond. If your spouse responds to the notice published in the newspaper, proceed with either the uncontested or contested procedure as necessary.

Special Circumstances 12

When You Can't Afford Court Costs

If you can't afford to pay the filing fee and other costs associated with the divorce, you will need to prepare and file a Petition to Sue/Appeal as an Indigent (Form 26). In order to qualify for a waiver of the filing fee, you must be indigent. If you are indigent, your income is probably low enough for you to qualify for public assistance (welfare).

> **Caution:** If you decide to use this form, you will probably be asked for more information to prove that you meet the requirements for being declared indigent, and therefore, eligible to have the filing and service fees waived. Before you file this form, you may want to see if the court clerk will give you any information on what is required to be declared indigent. You should also be aware that you can be held in contempt of court for giving false information on this form.

To complete the Petition to Sue/Appeal as an Indigent (Form 26) you need to:

1. Complete the top portion according to the instructions on page 62.
2. Place a check in the box beside the words "Petition to Sue."

3. Check the appropriate box to indicate whether or not you are receiving food stamps, AFDC or SSI.
4. Take the form to a notary and sign your name. You should also include your address below the signature box.

After you have completed the form take it to the Clerk's office when you file your DIVORCE COMPLAINT (Form 14) and CIVIL SUMMONS (Form 6). The clerk will decide whether or not you will need to pay the filing fee. If you are not receiving food stamps, AFDC, or SSI, the clerk is likely to insist that you complete an AFFIDAVIT OF INDIGENCY (Form 27).

To complete the AFFIDAVIT OF INDIGENCY (Form 27):

1. Complete the top portion according to the instructions on page 62.
2. Fill in your name, address, social security number and date of birth in the upper left hand portion of the form.
3. Fill in your monthly income and the name and address of your employer. (You do not need to include information on your spouse.)
4. Fill in your monthly expenses.
5. Fill in the information about your assets (the things or money you have) and liabilities (the debts or money you owe).
6. Take the form to a notary and sign and date the form on the back. In the space below the signature line, check the box and indicate you are the Plaintiff.

PROTECTING YOURSELF, YOUR CHILDREN, AND YOUR PROPERTY

Some people have three special concerns when getting prepared to file for a divorce: fear of physical attack by their spouse; fear their spouse will take and hide the children; and fear that their spouse will try to take the marital property and hide it. There are additional legal papers you can file if you feel you are in any of these situations.

PROTECTING YOURSELF

If you have a genuine fear that your spouse may attack you, you should go to the clerk's office and ask about filing papers to prevent domestic violence under section 50B-1 of the North Carolina General Statutes.

PROTECTING YOUR CHILDREN

If you are worried that your spouse may try to kidnap your children, then you should make sure that the day care center, baby-sitter, relative, or whomever you leave the children with at any time, is aware that you are in the process of a divorce and that the children are only to be released to you personally (not to your spouse or to any other relative, friend, etc.). To prevent your spouse from taking the children out of the United States, you can apply for a passport for each child. Once a passport is issued, the government will not issue another. So get their passport and lock it up in a safe deposit box. (This won't prevent them from being taken to Canada or Mexico, where passports are not required, but will prevent them from being taken overseas.) You can also file a motion to prevent the removal of the children from the state and to deny passport services. Forms for this motion are discussed at the beginning of appendix B, in the section titled WHERE TO FIND ADDITIONAL FORMS.

PROTECTING YOUR PROPERTY

If you genuinely fear that your spouse will try to remove money from bank accounts and try to hide important papers showing what property you own, you may want to take this same action before your spouse can. However, you can make a great deal of trouble for yourself with the judge if you do this to try to get these assets for yourself. So, make a complete list of any property you do take, and be sure to include these items in your FINANCIAL STATEMENT. You may need to convince the judge that you only took these items temporarily, in order to preserve them until a DIVORCE JUDGMENT is entered. Also, do not spend any cash you take from a bank account, or sell or give away any items of property you take. Any cash should be placed in a separate bank account, without your spouse's name on it, and kept separate from any other cash you have. Any papers, such as deeds, car titles, stock or bond certificates, etc., should be placed in a safe deposit box, without your spouse's name on it. The idea is not to take these things for yourself, but to get them in a safe place so your spouse can't hide them and deny they ever existed.

If your spouse is determined and resourceful, there is no guaranteed way to prevent the things discussed in this chapter from happening. All you can do is put as many obstacles in his or her way as possible, and prepare for him or her to suffer legal consequences for acting improperly.

Temporary Support and Custody

If your spouse has left you with the children, the mortgage, and monthly bills, and is not helping you out financially, you may want to consider asking the court to order the payment of support for you and the children during the divorce procedure. Of course, if you were the only person bringing in income and have been paying all the bills, don't expect to get any temporary support.

Obtaining temporary support or custody is a fairly complex procedure and will usually require the assistance of an attorney. This is particularly true if you need to obtain support or custody as an emergency measure without first notifying your spouse.

Taxes

As you are no doubt aware, the United States' income tax code is complicated and ever-changing. For this reason it is impossible to give detailed legal advice with respect to taxes in a book such as this. Any such information could easily be out of date by the time of publication. Therefore, it is strongly recommended that you consult your accountant, lawyer, or whomever prepares your tax return about the tax consequences of a divorce. A few general concerns are discussed in this chapter, to give you an idea of some of the tax questions that can arise.

Property and Taxes

You and your spouse may be exchanging title to property as a result of your divorce. Generally, there will not be any tax to pay as the result of such a transfer. However, whomever gets a piece of property will be responsible to pay any tax that may become due upon sale.

The Internal Revenue Service (I.R.S.) has issued numerous rulings about how property is to be treated in divorce situations. You need to be especially careful if you are transferring any tax shelters, or other complicated financial arrangements.

Be sure to read the following section on alimony, because fancy property settlements are asking for tax problems.

Child Support and Taxes

There are simple tax rules regarding child support:

1. Whoever has custody gets to claim the children on his or her tax return (unless both parents file a special I.R.S. form agreeing to a different arrangement each year).
2. The parent receiving child support does not need to report it as income.
3. The parent paying child support cannot deduct it.

If you are sharing physical custody, the parent with whom the child lives for the most time during the year is entitled to claim the child as a dependent.

The I.R.S. form to reverse this must be filed each year. Therefore, if you and your spouse have agreed that you will get to claim the children (even though you don't have custody), you should get your spouse to sign an open-ended form that you can file each year, so that you don't have to worry about it each year. A phone call to the I.R.S. can help you get answers to questions on this point.

Alimony and Taxes

Alimony can cause the most tax problems of any aspect of divorce. The I.R.S. is always making new rulings on whether an agreement is really alimony, or is really property division. The basic rule is that alimony is treated as income to the person receiving it, and as a deduction for the person paying it. Therefore, in order to manipulate the tax consequences, many couples try to show something as part of the property settlement, instead of as alimony; or the reverse. As the I.R.S. becomes aware of these "tax games" it issues rulings on how it will view a certain arrangement. If you are simply talking about the regular, periodic payment of cash, the I.R.S. will probably not question that it is alimony. (But if you try to call it a property settlement you may run into problems.) The important thing is to consult a tax expert if you are considering any unusual or creative property settlement or alimony arrangements.

Pension Plans

Pension plans, or retirement plans, for you and your spouse are marital assets, and may be very valuable assets. If you and your spouse are young, and have not been working very long, you may not have pension plans worth worrying about. Also, if you have both worked, and have similar pensions plans, it may be best just to include a provision in your settlement agreement that "each party shall keep his or her own pension plan." But if you have been married a long time, and your spouse worked while you stayed home to raise the children, your spouse's pension plan may be worth a lot of money, and may be necessary to see you through retirement. If you and your spouse cannot agree on how to divide a pension plan, you should see an attorney. The valuation of pension plans, and how they are to be divided, is a complicated matter that you should not attempt.

Appendix A
General Statutes of North Carolina and Child Support Guidelines

This appendix contains selected portions of the General Statutes of North Carolina relating to divorce, and the North Carolina Child Support Guidelines. For further information, review the section on LEGAL RESEARCH in chapter 2 of this book.

GENERAL STATUTES OF NORTH CAROLINA

§ 50-6. Divorce after separation of one year on application of either party.

Marriages may be dissolved and the parties thereto divorced from the bonds of matrimony on the application of either party, if and when the husband and wife have lived separate and apart for one year, and the plaintiff or defendant in the suit for divorce has resided in the State for a period of six months. A divorce under this section shall not be barred to either party by any defense or plea based upon any provision of G.S. 50-7, a plea of res judicata, or a plea of recrimination. Notwithstanding the provisions of G.S. 50-11, or the common law, a divorce under this section shall not affect the rights of a dependent spouse with respect to alimony which have been asserted in the action or any other pending action.

Whether there has been a resumption of marital relations during the period of separation shall be determined pursuant to G.S. 52-10.2. Isolated incidents of sexual intercourse between the parties shall not toll the statutory period required for divorce predicated on separation of one year.

§ 50-7. Grounds for divorce from bed and board.

The court may grant divorces from bed and board on application of the party injured, made as by law provided, in the following cases if either party:

(1) Abandons his or her family.
(2) Maliciously turns the other out of doors.
(3) By cruel or barbarous treatment endangers the life of the other. In addition, the court may grant the victim of such treatment the remedies available under G.S. 50B-1, et seq.
(4) Offers such indignities to the person of the other as to render his or her condition intolerable and life burdensome.
(5) Becomes an excessive user of alcohol or drugs so as to render the condition of the other spouse intolerable and the life of that spouse burdensome.
(6) Commits adultery.

§ 50-12. Resumption of maiden name or adoption of name of prior deceased or prior divorced husband.

(a) Any woman whose marriage is dissolved by a decree of absolute divorce may, upon application to the clerk of court of the county in which she resides setting forth her intention to do so, change her name to any of the following:

(1) Her maiden name; or
(2) The surname of a prior deceased husband; or
(3) The surname of a prior husband if she has children who have that husband's surname.

[*Subparagraphs (b) and (c) are deleted.*]

(d) In the complaint, or counterclaim for divorce filed by any woman in this State, she may petition the court to adopt any surname as provided by this section, and the court is authorized to incorporate in the divorce decree an order authorizing her to adopt that surname.

§ 50-13.2. Who entitled to custody; terms of custody; visitation rights of grandparents; taking child out of State.

(a) An order for custody of a minor child entered pursuant to this section shall award the custody of such child to such person, agency, organization or institution as will best promote the interest and welfare of the child. An order for custody must include findings of fact which support the determination of what is in the best interest of the child. Between the mother and father, whether natural or adoptive, no presumptions shall apply as to who will better promote the interest and welfare of the child. Joint custody to the parents shall be considered upon the request of either parent.

(b) An order for custody of a minor child may grant joint custody to the parents, exclusive custody to one person, agency, organization, or institution, or grant custody to two of more persons, agencies, organizations, or institutions. Any order for custody shall include such terms, including visitation, as will best promote the interest and welfare of the child. Absent an order of the court to the contrary, each parent shall have equal access to the records of the minor child involving the health, education, and welfare of the child.

(b1) An order for custody of a minor child may provide visitation rights for any grandparent of the child as the court, in its discretion, deems appropriate. As used in this subsection, "grandparent" includes a biological grandparent of a child adopted by a stepparent or a relative of the child where a substantial relationship exists between the grandparent and the child. Under no circumstances shall a biological grandparent of a child adopted by adoptive parents, neither of whom is related to the child and where parental rights of both biological parents have been terminated, be entitled to visitation rights.

(c) An order for custody of a minor child may provide for such child to be taken outside of the State, but if the order contemplates the return of the child to this State, the judge may require the person, agency, organization or institution having custody out of the State to give bond or other security conditioned upon the return of the child to this State in accordance with the order of the court.

(d) If, within a reasonable time, one parent fails to consent to adoption pursuant to Chapter 48 of the General Statutes or parental rights have not been terminated, the consent of the other consenting parent shall not be effective in an action for custody of the child.

§ 50-16.1A. Definitions.

As used in this Chapter, unless the context clearly requires otherwise, the following definitions apply:

(1) "Alimony" means an order for payment for the support and maintenance of a spouse or former spouse, periodically or in a lump sum, for a specified or for an indefinite term, ordered in an action for divorce, whether absolute or from bed and board, or in an action for alimony without divorce.
(2) "Dependent spouse" means a spouse, whether husband or wife, who is actually substantially dependent upon the other spouse for his or her maintenance and support or is substantial in need of maintenance and support from the other spouse.
(3) "Marital misconduct" means any of the following acts that occur during the marriage and prior to or on the date of separation:
    a. Illicit sexual behavior. For the purpose of this section, illicit sexual behavior means acts of sexual or deviate sexual intercourse, deviate sexual acts, or

sexual acts defined in G.S. 14-27.1(4), voluntarily engaged in by a spouse with someone other than the other spouse;
b. Involuntary separation of the spouses in consequence of a criminal act committed prior to the proceeding in which alimony is sought;
c. Abandonment of the other spouse;
d. Malicious turning out-of-doors of the other spouse;
e. Cruel or barbarous treatment endangering the life of the other spouse;
f. Indignities rendering the condition of the other spouse intolerable and life burdensome;
g. Reckless spending of the income of either party, or the destruction, waste, diversion, or concealment of assets;
h. Excessive use of alcohol or drugs so as to render the condition of the other spouse intolerable and life burdensome.
i. Willful failure to provide necessary subsistence according to one's means and condition so as to render the condition of the other spouse intolerable and life burdensome.

(4) "Postseparation support" means spousal support to be paid until the earlier of either the date specified in the order of postseparation support, or an order awarding or denying alimony. Postseparation support may be ordered in an action for divorce, whether absolute or from bed and board, for annulment, or for alimony without divorce.

(5) "Supporting spouse" means a spouse, whether husband or wife, upon whom the other spouse is actually substantially dependent for maintenance and support or from whom such spouse is substantially in need of maintenance and support.

§ 50.16.2A. Postseparation support.

(a) In an action brought pursuant to Chapter 50 of the General Statutes, either party may move for postseparation support. The verified pleading, verified motion, or affidavit of the moving party shall set forth the factual basis for the relief requested.

(b) In ordering postseparation support, the court shall base its award on the financial needs of the parties, considering the parties' accustomed standard of living, the present employment income and other recurring earnings of each party from any source, their income-earning abilities, the separate and marital debt service obligations, those expenses reasonably necessary to support each of the parties, and each party's respective legal obligations to support any other persons.

(c) Except when subsection (d) of this section applies, a dependent spouse is entitled to an award of postseparation support if, based on consideration of the factors specified in subsection (b) of this section, the court finds that the resources of the dependent spouse are not adequate to meet his or her reasonable needs and the supporting spouse has the ability to pay.

(d) At a hearing on postseparation support, the judge shall consider marital misconduct by the dependent spouse occurring prior to or on the date of separation in deciding whether to award postseparation support and in deciding the amount of postseparation support. When the judge considers these acts by the dependent spouse, the judge shall also consider any marital misconduct by the supporting spouse in deciding whether to award postseparation support and in deciding the amount of postseparation support.

(e) Nothing herein shall prevent a court from considering incidents of post date-of-separation marital misconduct as corroborating evidence supporting other evidence that marital misconduct occurred during the marriage and prior to date of separation.

§ 50.16.3A. Alimony.

(a) Entitlement.—In an action brought pursuant to Chapter 50 of the General Statutes, either party may move for alimony. The court shall award alimony to the dependent spouse upon a finding that one spouse is a dependent spouse, that the other spouse is a supporting spouse, and that an award of alimony is equitable after considering all relevant factors, including those set out in subsection (b) of this section. If the court finds that the dependent spouse participated in an act of illicit sexual behavior, as defined in G.S. 50-16.1A(3)a., during the marriage and prior to or on the date of separation, then the court shall order that alimony be paid to a dependent spouse. If the court finds that the dependent and the supporting spouse each participated in an act of illicit sexual behavior during the marriage and prior to or on the date of separation, then alimony shall be denied or awarded in the discretion of the court after consideration of all of the circumstances. Any act of illicit sexual behavior by either party that has been condoned by the other party shall not be considered by the court.

The claim for alimony may be heard on the merits prior to the entry of a judgment for equitable distribution, and if awarded, the issues of amount and of whether a spouse is a dependent spouse may be reviewed by the court after the conclusion of the equitable distribution claim.

(b) Amount and Duration.—The court shall exercise its discretion in determining the amount, duration, and manner of payment of alimony. The duration of the award may be for a specified or for an indefinite term. In determining the amount, duration, and manner of payment of alimony, the court shall consider all relevant factors, including:

(1) The marital misconduct of either of the spouses. Nothing herein shall prevent a court from considering incidents of post date-of-separation marital misconduct as corroborating evidence supporting other evidence that marital misconduct occurred during the marriage and prior to date of separation;
(2) The relative earnings and earning capacities of the spouses;
(3) The ages and the physical, mental, and emotional conditions of the spouses;
(4) The amount and sources of earned and unearned income of both spouses, including, but not limited to, earnings, dividends, and benefits such as medical, retirement, insurance, social security, or others;
(5) The duration of the marriage;
(6) The contribution by one spouse to the education, training, or increased earning power of the other spouse;
(7) The extent to which the earning power, expenses, or financial obligations of a spouse will be affected by reason of serving as the custodian of a minor child;
(8) The standard of living of the spouses established during the marriage;
(9) The relative education of the spouses and the time necessary to acquire sufficient education or training to enable the spouse seeking alimony to find employment to meet his or her reasonable economic needs;
(10) The relative assets and liabilities of the spouses and the relative debt service requirements of the spouses, including legal obligations of support;
(11) The property brought to the marriage by either spouse;
(12) The contribution of a spouse as homemaker;
(13) The relative needs of the spouses;
(14) The federal, State, and local tax ramifications of the alimony award;
(15) Any other factor relating to the economic circumstances of the parties that the court finds to be just and proper.

(c) Findings of Fact.—The court shall set forth the reasons for its award or denial of alimony and, if making an award, the reasons for its amount, duration, and manner of payment. Except where there is a motion before the court for summary judgment, judgment on the pleadings, or other motion for which the Rules of Civil Procedure do not require special findings of fact, the court shall make a specific finding of fact on each of the factors in subsection (b) of this section if evidence is offered on that factor.

(d) In the claims for alimony, either spouse may request a jury trial on the issue of marital misconduct as defined in G.S. 50-16.1A. If a jury trial is requested, the jury will decide whether either spouse or both have established marital misconduct.

§ 50.16.8. Procedure in actions for postseparation support.

When an application is made for postseparation support, the court may base its award on a verified pleading, affidavit, or other competent evidence. The court shall set forth the reasons for its award or denial of postseparation support, and if making an award, the reasons for its amount, duration, and manner of payment.

§ 50-20. Distribution by court of marital property upon divorce.

[*Subsection (a) deleted.*]

(b) For purposes of this section:
(1) "Marital property" means all real and personal property acquired by either spouse or both spouses during the course of the mar-

riage and before the date of the separation of the parties, and presently owned, except property determined to be separate property in accordance with subdivision (2) of this section. Marital property includes all vested pension, retirement, and other deferred compensation rights, including military pensions eligible under the federal Uniformed Services Former Spouses' Protection Act.

(2) "Separate property" means all real and personal property acquired by a spouse before marriage or acquired by a spouse by bequest, devise, descent, or gift during the course of the marriage. However, property acquired by gift from the other spouse during the course of the marriage shall be considered separate property only if such an intention is stated in the conveyance. Property acquired in exchange for separate property shall remain separate property regardless of whether the title is in the name of the husband or wife or both and shall not be considered to be marital property unless a contrary intention is expressly stated in the conveyance. The increase in value of separate property and the income derived from separate property shall be considered separate property. All professional licenses and business licenses which would terminate on transfer shall be considered separate property. The expectation of nonvested pension, retirement, or other deferred compensation rights shall be considered separate property.

[*Subsection (3) deleted.*]

(c) There shall be an equal division by using net value of marital property unless the court determines that an equal division is not equitable. If the court determines that an equal division is not equitable, the court shall divide the marital property equitably. Factors the court shall consider under this subsection are as follows:

(1) The income, property, and liabilities of each party at the time the division of property is to become effective;

(2) Any obligation for support arising out of a prior marriage;

(3) The duration of the marriage and the age and physical and mental health of both parties;

(4) The need of a parent with custody of a child or children of the marriage to occupy or own the marital residence and to use or own its household effects;

(5) The expectation of nonvested pension, retirement, or other deferred compensation rights, which is separate property;

(6) Any equitable claim to, interest in, or direct or indirect contribution made to the acquisition of such marital property by the party not having title, including joint efforts or expenditures and contributions and services, or lack thereof, as a spouse, parent, wage earner or homemaker;

(7) Any direct or indirect contribution made by one spouse to help educate or develop the career potential of the other spouse;

(8) Any direct contribution to an increase in value of separate property which occurs during the course of the marriage;

(9) The liquid or nonliquid character of all marital property;

(10) The difficulty of evaluating any component asset or any interest in a business, corporation or profession, and the economic desirability of retaining such asset or interest, intact and free from any claim or interference by the other party;

(11) The tax consequences to each party;

(11a) Acts of either party to maintain, preserve, develop, or expand; or to waste, neglect, devalue or convert such marital property, during the period after separation of the parties and before the time of distribution; and

(12) Any other factor which the court finds to be just and proper.

[*Subparagraphs (d) through (K) are deleted.*]

CHILD SUPPORT GUIDELINES

Below and on the following ten pages, you will find the North Carolina Child Support Guidelines, which include the child support tables you will use to calculate child support if you have minor children. These guidelines are taken from the official North Carolina form. Read these guidelines carefully. The child support tables indicate an effective date of October 1, 1994, which is the most current version as of the date this book is being published. The law provides that these guidelines must be reviewed, and modified if necessary, at least every four years.

NORTH CAROLINA CHILD SUPPORT GUIDELINES

Effective October 1, 1998

Commentary

North Carolina G.S. 50-13.4 provides that the Conference of Chief District Judges prescribe uniform statewide presumptive guidelines for the computation of child support obligations of each parent. The statute further provides that the Conference periodically, but at least once every four years, review the guidelines to determine whether their application results in appropriate child support award amounts, and modify the guidelines accordingly.

The North Carolina Child Support Guidelines are based on the Income Share model, which was developed under the Child Support Guidelines Project funded by the U.S. Office of Child Support Enforcement and administered by the National Center for State Courts. The Income Shares model is based on the concept that child support is a shared parental obligation and that a child should receive the same proportion of parental income he or she would have received if the parents lived together. The Schedule of Basic Child Support Obligations is based primarily on economic research performed pursuant to the Family Support Obligations is based primarily on economic research performed pursuant to the Family Support Act of 1988 [P.L. 100-485, § 128] which required the U.S. Department of Health and Human Services to conduct a study of the patterns of expenditures on children. The schedule has been updated using changes in the Consumer Price Index.

The Guidelines contained herein are the product of the ongoing review process conducted by the Conference of Chief District Judges. A public hearing was conducted by the Conference to provide interested citizens an opportunity to comment on the Guidelines, and written comment was received from agencies, attorneys, judges and members of the public. These Guidelines are intended to provide adequate awards of child support which are equitable to all parties.

The North Carolina Child Support Guidelines, promulgated by the Conference of Chief District Judges, are published by the North Carolina Administrative Office of the Courts and the Department of Health and Human Services in accordance with G.S. 60-13.4(c). Additional copies of these Guidelines and worksheets for applying the guidelines are available from the offices of the Clerk of the Superior COurt. For information regarding the use of the Child Support Guidelines, please refer to G.S. 50-13.4(c).

NORTH CAROLINA CHILD SUPPORT GUIDELINES

Pursuant to G.S. 50-13.4(c), the North Carolina Child Support Guidelines apply as a rebuttable presumption to all child support orders in North Carolina, except as discussed below. The Guidelines must be used for temporary and permanent child support orders. The Guidelines must be used by the Court as the basis for reviewing the adequacy of child support levels in non-contested cases as well as contested hearings. The Court upon its own motion or upon motion of a party may deviate from the Guidelines in cases where application would be inequitable to one of the parties or the child(ren). If the Court orders an amount other than the amount determined by application of the Guidelines, the Court must make written findings of fact that justify the deviation, that state the amount of the award which would have resulted from the application of the Guidelines, and that justify the amount of support awarded by the Court.

Self-Support Reserve; Obligors With Low Incomes

The Guidelines include a self support reserve which ensures that obligors have sufficient income to maintain a minimum standard of living based on the 1997 federal poverty level for one person. For obligors with an adjusted gross income of less than $800, the Guidelines require, absent a deviation, the establishment of a minimum support order ($50). For obligors with adjusted gross incomes above $800, the Schedule of Basic Support Obligations incorporates a further adjustment to maintain the self support reserve for the obligor.

If the obligor's adjusted gross income falls within the shaded area of Schedule, the basic child support obligation and the obligor's total child support obligation are computed using only the obligor's income. This approach prevents disproportionate increases in the child support obligation with moderate increases in income and protects the integrity of the self support reserve. In all other cases, the basic child support obligation is computed using the combined adjusted incomes of both parents.

Determination of Support in Cases Involving High Combined Incomes

The Guidelines apply in cases in which the parents' combined adjusted gross income is equal to or less than $15,000 per month ($180,000 per year). For cases with higher combined adjusted gross income, child support should be determined on a case-by-case basis, provided that the amount of support awarded may not be lower than the maximum basic child support obligation shown in the Schedule of Basic Child Support Obligations.

Assumptions and Expenses included in Schedule of Basic Child Support Obligations

The Schedule is based on economic date which represent estimated of total expenditures on child rearing costs to age 18, except for child care, health insurance, and health care costs in excess of $100 per year. Expenses incurred in the exercise of visitation are not factored into the Schedule.

The Schedule presumes that the custodial parent claims the tax exemptions for child(ren) due support. If the custodial parent has no income tax liability, the Court may consider assigning the exemption for the child(ren) to the non-custodial parent, and deviate from the Guidelines by increasing the obligor's support obligation.

Income

The Schedule of Basic Child Support Obligations is based upon the net income converted to gross annual income for ease of application.

For the purpose of these Guidelines, "income" is defines as actual gross income of the parent, if employed to full capacity, or potential income if unemployed or underemployed. All income is assumed to be taxable. Gross income of each parent should be determined as specified below.

(1) Gross income: Gross income includes income from any source, except as excluded below, and includes but is not limited to income from salaries, wages, commissions, bonuses, dividends, severance pay, pensions, interest, trust income, annuities, capital gains, social security benefits, workers' compensation benefits, unemployment insurance benefits, disability pay and insurance benefits, gifts, prizes and alimony or maintenance received from persons other than the parties to the instant action. While includable as income, non-recurring one-time payments should be distinguished from ongoing income.

Specifically excluded are benefits received from means-tested public assistance programs, including but not limited to Aid to Families with Dependent Children (AFDC), Supplemental Security Income (SSI), Food Stamps and General Assistance.

Payments received for the benefits of the child(ren) as a result of the disability of the obligor are not considered in determining the amount of the basic child support obligation. However, after determining the amount of the obligor's support obligation under the Guidelines, the Court should compare the obligor's support obligation under the guidelines with the benefits received by the child(ren) due to the obligor's disability, and determine whether an award of child support in addition to the child(ren) disability-related benefits is warranted.

(2) Income from self-employment or operation of a business: For income from self-employment, rent, royalties, proprietorship of a business, or joint ownership of a partnership or closely held corporation, gross income is defined as gross receipts minus ordinary and necessary expenses required for self-employment or business operation. Specifically excluded from ordinary and necessary expenses for purposes of these Guidelines are amounts allowable by the Internal Revenue Service for the accelerated component of depreciation expenses, investment tax credits, or any other business expenses determined by the Court to be inappropriate for determining gross income for purposes of calculating child support. In general, income and expenses from self-employment or operation of a business should be carefully reviewed to determine an appropriate level of gross income available to the parent to satisfy a child support obligation. In most cases, this amount will differ from a determination of business income for tax purposes.

Expanse reimbursements or in-kind payments received by a parent in the course of employment, self-employment, or operation of a business should be counted as income if they are significant and reduce personal living expenses. Such payments might include a company car, free housing, or reimbursed meals.

(3) Potential income: If a parent is voluntarily unemployed or underemployed, child support may be calculated based on a determination of potential income, except that a determination of potential income should not be made for a parent who is physically or mentally incapacitated or is caring for a child who is under the age of thee years and for whom the parents owe a joint legal responsibility.

Determination of potential income shall be made by determining employment potential and probable earnings level is based on the parent's recent work history, occupational qualifications and prevailing job opportunities and earning levels in the community. If the parent has no recent work history, and/or vocational training, it is suggested that the Court determine potential income in an amount not less than the minimum hourly wage for a 40-hour work week.

In each a case, the Court should consider the prior circumstances of the parties in determining whether or not to impute income.

(4) Income verification: Income statements of the parents should be verified with documentation of both current and past income. Suitable documentation of current earnings (at least one full month) includes pay stubs, employer statements, or receipts and expenses if self-employed. Documentation of current income must be supplemented with copies of the most recent tax return to provide verification of earnings over a longer period. Sanctions may be imposed for failure to comply with this provision on the motion of either party or by the Court on its own motion.

Pre-existing Child Support Obligations and Responsibility for Other Child(ren)

The amount of child support payments actually made by a party under any pre-existing court order(s) or separation agreement(s) should be deducted from the party's gross income. Actual payments of alimony should not be considered as deduction from gross income but may be considered as a factor to vary from the final presumptive child support obligation.

Th amount of a party's financial responsibility (as determined below) for his or her natural or adopted child(ren) currently residing in the household who are not involved in this action should be deducted from gross income. Use of this deduction is appropriate at the time of the establishment of a child support in a proceeding to modify an existing order. However, in a proceeding to modify, it may not be the sole basis for a reduction.

The deduction for a party's financial responsibility for other child(ren) is one-half of the basic child support obligation for the number of child(ren) who live with the party and for whom the party owes a duty of support (other than the child(ren) involved in the instant action). For purposes of this deduction, the basic child support obligation for the other child(ren) living with the party is based on the combined adjusted gross incomes of the party and the other responsible parent of such child(ren).

Basic Child Support Obligation

The basic child support obligation is determined using the attached Schedule of Basic Child Support Obligations. For combined monthly adjusted gross income amounts falling between amounts shown in the Schedule, the basic child support obligation should be interpolated.

The number of child(ren) refers to child(ren) for whom the parents share joint legal responsibility and for whom support is being sought.

Child Care Costs

Reasonable child care costs incurred due to employment or job search are added to the basic obligation as follows:

(1) When the gross monthly income of the party paying such costs falls below the level indicated below, 100% of child care costs are added.

1 child	= $1,100	4 children	= $1,900
2 children	= $1,500	5 children	= $2,100
3 children	= $1,700	6 children	= $2,300

At these income levels, the party paying child care costs does not benefit from the tax credit for child care.

(2) When the income of the party exceeds the level indicated above, 75% of child care costs are included since the party would be entitled to the income tax credit for child care expenses.

Health Insurance

The cost of health care (medical, or medical and dental insurance for the child(ren) due support is added to the basic child support obligation. The amount included in the child support calculation in the amount of health insurance premium actually attributable to the child(ren) subject to the order. If this amount is not available or cannot be verified, the total cost of premium is divided by the total number of persons covered by the policy and then multiplied by the number of child(ren) covered by the policy who are subject tot he order.

If coverage is provided through an employer, only the employee's portion of costs should be considered. Medical or dental expenses in excess of $100 per year and uncompensated by insurance should be divided between the parties in proportion to their respective incomes.

Extraordinary Expenses

The Court may make adjustments for extraordinary expenses and order payments for such term and in such manner as the Court deems necessary. Extraordinary medical expenses are uninsured expenses in excess of $100 for a single illness or condition. Extraordinary medical expenses include, but are not limited to, such costs as are reasonably necessary for orthodontia, dental treatments, asthma treatments, physical therapy and any uninsured chronic health problem. At the discretion of the4 Court, professional counseling or psychiatric therapy for diagnosed mental disorders may also be considered as an extraordinary medical expense. Payments for such expenses shall be apportioned in the same manner as the basic child support obligation and ordered paid as the Court deems equitable.

Other extraordinary expenses are added to the basic child support obligation. Other extraordinary expenses include:

(1) Any expenses for attending any special or private elementary or secondary schools to meet the particular educational needs of the child(ren); (2) Any expenses for transportation of the child(ren) between the homes of the parents.

Determination of Child Support Obligation and Presumptive Award

Except in cases in which the obligor's income falls within the shaded area of the Schedule, the non-custodial parent's total child support obligation is determined by adding the basic child support obligation plus the amount of work-related child care costs, health insurance premiums for the child(ren), and extraordinary expenses. The non-custodial parent's total child support obligation is determined by multiplying the total child support obligation by the non-custodial parent's percentage of combined adjusted income. The non-custodial parent receives credit for the amount of child care costs, health insurance premiums, and extraordinary expenses that he or she pays out-of-pocket. The recommended child support order is determined by subtracting the amount of child care costs, health insurance premiums for the child(ren), and extraordinary expenses paid by the non-custodial parent's total child support obligation.

Modification

In any proceeding to modify an existing order which is three years old or older, a deviation of 15% or more between the amount of the existing order and the amount of child support resulting from application of the Guidelines shall be presumed to constitute a substantial change of circumstances warranting modification. If the order is less than three years old, this presumption does not apply.

North Carolina

Proposed Monthly Basic Child Support Obligations

Combined Gross Monthly Income	Effective October 1, 1998					
	One Child	Two Children	Three Children	Four Children	Five Children	Six Children
0-800	50	50	50	50	50	50
850	68	69	69	70	71	72
900	100	101	102	103	104	105
950	132	134	135	136	138	139
1000	164	166	168	170	171	173
1050	196	198	201	203	205	207
1100	223	231	233	236	239	241
1150	232	263	266	269	272	275
1200	240	296	299	302	306	309
1250	249	328	332	336	339	343
1300	258	361	365	369	373	377
1350	266	387	398	402	406	411
1400	274	399	430	435	440	444
1450	282	411	463	468	473	478
1500	290	422	496	501	507	512
1550	298	434	513	534	540	546
1600	306	445	527	567	573	579
1650	314	457	540	597	606	613
1700	322	468	554	612	639	646
1750	330	480	567	627	672	679
1800	338	491	581	642	696	713
1850	346	503	594	657	712	746
1900	354	514	608	672	728	779
1950	362	526	621	686	744	796
2000	370	538	635	701	760	814
Pablo's 2004 ◀ 2050	(87/wk) 378	549	648	716	777	831
2100	386	561	662	731	793	848
2150	394	572	675	746	809	866
2200	402	584	689	761	825	883
2250	410	595	702	776	841	900
2300	418	607	716	791	858	918
2350	426	618	730	806	874	935
2400	434	630	743	821	890	952
2450	442	641	757	836	906	970
2500	450	653	770	851	922	987
2550	458	664	783	865	938	1004
2600	465	675	796	880	953	1020
2650	472	685	807	892	967	1035
2700	479	694	818	904	980	1048
2750	485	703	829	916	992	1062
2800	492	712	839	927	1005	1075
2850	498	721	850	939	1018	1089

AOC-A-162, Page 5 of 12
Rev. 10/94

Combined Gross Monthly Income	Effective October 1, 1998					
	One Child	Two Children	Three Children	Four Children	Five Children	Six Children
2900	504	730	860	950	1030	1102
2950	511	740	871	962	1043	1116
2001-2003 3000	(117/wk) 517	749	881	974	1055	1129
3050	524	758	892	985	1068	1143
3100	530	767	902	997	1081	1156
3150	536	776	913	1008	1093	1170
3200	543	785	923	1020	1106	1183
3250	549	794	934	1032	1119	1197
☆ 3300	555	803	945	1044	1131	1211
3350	561	812	955	1056	1144	1224
ombined 2004 ☆ 3400	(130/wk) 567	821	966	1068	1157	1238
3450	574	830	977	1079	1170	1252
3500	580	839	988	1091	1183	1266
3550	586	848	998	1103	1196	1280
3600	592	857	1009	1115	1209	1293
3650	598	866	1020	1127	1222	1307
3700	604	875	1031	1139	1234	1321
3750	610	884	1041	1151	1247	1335
3800	617	893	1052	1163	1260	1348
3850	623	902	1063	1174	1273	1362
3900	629	911	1074	1186	1286	1376
3950	635	920	1084	1198	1299	1390
4000	638	925	1090	1205	1306	1397
4050	642	930	1096	1211	1312	1404
4100	645	934	1101	1217	1319	1411
4150	648	939	1106	1222	1325	1418
4200	652	944	1112	1228	1331	1425
4250	655	948	1117	1234	1338	1432
4300	658	953	1122	1240	1344	1438
4350	662	958	1128	1246	1351	1445
4400	665	962	1133	1252	1357	1452
4450	668	967	1138	1258	1363	1459
4500	671	972	1144	1264	1370	1466
4550	675	976	1149	1270	1376	1473
4600	678	981	1154	1276	1383	1479
4650	682	987	1162	1284	1392	1489
4700	684	990	1165	1287	1395	1493
4750	686	993	1168	1290	1399	1496
4800	688	997	1171	1293	1402	1500
4850	691	1000	1173	1297	1406	1504
4900	693	1004	1176	1300	1409	1508
4950	695	1007	1179	1303	1413	1511
5000	697	1010	1182	1306	1416	1515
5050	699	1014	1185	1310	1420	1519
5100	701	1017	1188	1313	1423	1523
5150	703	1020	1191	1316	1426	1526

Combined Gross Monthly Income	Effective October 1, 1998					
	One Child	Two Children	Three Children	Four Children	Five Children	Six Children
5200	705	1024	1194	1319	1430	1530
5250	707	1027	1196	1322	1433	1533
5300	709	1030	1199	1325	1436	1537
5350	711	1033	1202	1328	1440	1540
5400	713	1036	1205	1331	1443	1544
5450	715	1040	1207	1334	1446	1547
5500	720	1047	1216	1344	1457	1559
5550	725	1053	1225	1354	1467	1570
5600	730	1060	1234	1363	1478	1581
5650	736	1067	1243	1373	1488	1593
5700	741	1074	1251	1383	1499	1604
5750	746	1081	1260	1393	1509	1615
5800	752	1088	1269	1402	1520	1626
5850	757	1095	1278	1412	1531	1638
5900	762	1101	1287	1422	1541	1649
5950	768	1108	1295	1431	1552	1660
6000	773	1115	1304	1441	1562	1672
6050	778	1122	1313	1451	1573	1683
6100	783	1129	1322	1461	1583	1694
6150	789	1136	1331	1470	1594	1706
6200	793	1142	1338	1479	1603	1715
6250	797	1148	1345	1487	1612	1724
6300	802	1154	1353	1495	1620	1734
6350	806	1160	1360	1502	1629	1743
6400	810	1167	1367	1510	1637	1752
6450	814	1173	1374	1518	1646	1761
6500	818	1179	1381	1526	1654	1770
6550	823	1185	1388	1534	1663	1779
6600	827	1191	1396	1542	1672	1789
6650	831	1197	1403	1550	1680	1798
6700	835	1203	1410	1558	1689	1807
6750	840	1209	1417	1566	1697	1816
6800	844	1215	1424	1574	1706	1825
6850	848	1222	1431	1582	1715	1835
6900	852	1228	1439	1590	1723	1844
6950	857	1234	1446	1598	1732	1853
7000	861	1240	1453	1606	1740	1862
7050	865	1246	1460	1613	1749	1871
7100	869	1252	1467	1621	1758	1881
7150	873	1258	1475	1629	1766	1890
7200	878	1264	1482	1637	1775	1899
7250	882	1270	1489	1645	1783	1908
7300	886	1276	1496	1653	1791	1917
7350	890	1282	1502	1660	1800	1926
7400	894	1288	1509	1668	1808	1934
7450	898	1294	1516	1675	1816	1943
7500	902	1300	1523	1683	1824	1952
7550	907	1306	1530	1690	1832	1961
7600	911	1312	1537	1698	1841	1969
7650	915	1317	1543	1706	1849	1978

Combined Gross Monthly Income	Effective October 1, 1998					
	One Child	Two Children	Three Children	Four Children	Five Children	Six Children
7700	919	1323	1550	1713	1857	1987
7750	923	1329	1557	1721	1865	1996
7800	927	1335	1564	1728	1873	2005
7850	931	1341	1571	1736	1882	2013
7900	935	1347	1578	1743	1890	2022
7950	940	1353	1585	1751	1898	2031
8000	944	1359	1591	1759	1906	2040
8050	948	1365	1598	1766	1914	2048
8100	952	1370	1605	1774	1923	2057
8150	956	1376	1612	1781	1931	2066
8200	960	1382	1619	1789	1939	2075
8250	964	1388	1626	1796	1947	2084
8300	968	1394	1633	1804	1956	2092
8350	973	1400	1639	1812	1964	2101
8400	977	1406	1646	1819	1972	2110
8450	981	1412	1653	1827	1980	2119
8500	985	1418	1660	1834	1988	2128
8550	989	1423	1667	1842	1997	2136
8600	993	1429	1674	1849	2005	2145
8650	997	1435	1681	1857	2013	2154
8700	1001	1441	1687	1865	2021	2163
8750	1006	1447	1694	1872	2030	2172
8800	1010	1453	1701	1880	2038	2180
8850	1014	1459	1708	1886	2046	2189
8900	1018	1465	1715	1895	2054	2198
8950	1022	1471	1722	1903	2063	2207
9000	1026	1477	1729	1910	2071	2216
9050	1030	1482	1736	1918	2079	2225
9100	1034	1488	1743	1926	2087	2234
9150	1038	1494	1750	1933	2096	2242
9200	1043	1500	1757	1941	2104	2251
9250	1047	1506	1763	1949	2112	2260
9300	1051	1512	1770	1956	2121	2269
9350	1055	1518	1777	1964	2129	2278
9400	1059	1524	1784	1972	2137	2287
9450	1063	1530	1791	1979	2145	2296
9500	1067	1536	1798	1987	2154	2304
9550	1071	1541	1805	1994	2162	2313
9600	1075	1547	1812	2002	2170	2322
9650	1080	1553	1819	2010	2179	2331
9700	1084	1559	1826	2017	2187	2340
9750	1088	1565	1833	2025	2195	2349
9800	1092	1571	1839	2033	2203	2358
9850	1096	1577	1846	2040	2212	2366
9900	1100	1583	1853	2048	2220	2375

Combined Gross Monthly Income	Effective October 1, 1998					
	One Child	Two Children	Three Children	Four Children	Five Children	Six Children
9950	1104	1589	1860	2056	2228	2384
10000	1108	1595	1867	2063	2236	2393
10050	1112	1601	1874	2071	2245	2402
10100	1116	1607	1881	2079	2254	2411
10150	1121	1613	1889	2087	2262	2421
10200	1125	1619	1896	2095	2271	2430
10250	1129	1625	1904	2104	2280	2440
10300	1133	1631	1911	2112	2289	2449
10350	1137	1637	1918	2120	2298	2459
10400	1141	1643	1926	2128	2307	2468
10450	1145	1649	1933	2136	2316	2478
10500	1149	1655	1941	2144	2325	2487
10550	1153	1661	1948	2153	2333	2497
10600	1157	1667	1956	2161	2342	2506
10650	1161	1674	1963	2169	2351	2516
10700	1165	1680	1970	2177	2360	2525
10750	1169	1686	1978	2185	2369	2535
10800	1173	1692	1985	2194	2378	2544
10850	1177	1698	1993	2202	2387	2554
10900	1181	1704	2000	2210	2396	2563
10950	1185	1710	2007	2218	2405	2573
11000	1189	1716	2014	2226	2413	2582
11050	1193	1721	2021	2233	2421	2590
11100	1197	1727	2028	2241	2429	2599
11150	1200	1732	2035	2248	2437	2608
11200	1204	1738	2041	2256	2445	2616
11250	1208	1744	2048	2263	2453	2625
11300	1212	1749	2055	2271	2462	2634
11350	1215	1755	2062	2278	2470	2643
11400	1219	1760	2069	2286	2478	2651
11450	1223	1766	2075	2293	2486	2660
11500	1226	1772	2082	2301	2494	2669
11550	1229	1775	2087	2306	2499	2674
11600	1231	1778	2090	2310	2504	2679
11650	1233	1781	2094	2314	2508	2684
11700	1235	1784	2097	2318	2512	2688
11750	1237	1787	2101	2322	2517	2693
11800	1238	1790	2105	2326	2521	2697
11850	1240	1793	2108	2330	2525	2702
11900	1242	1796	2112	2334	2530	2707
11950	1244	1799	2115	2338	2534	2711

Combined Gross Monthly Income	Effective October 1, 1998					
	One Child	Two Children	Three Children	Four Children	Five Children	Six Children
12000	1246	1801	2119	2342	2538	2716
12050	1248	1804	2123	2345	2543	2720
12100	1250	1807	2126	2349	2547	2725
12150	1252	1810	2130	2353	2551	2730
12200	1254	1813	2133	2357	2555	2734
12250	1256	1816	2137	2361	2560	2739
12300	1258	1819	2141	2365	2564	2744
12350	1260	1822	2144	2369	2568	2748
12400	1262	1825	2148	2373	2573	2753
12450	1264	1828	2151	2377	2577	2757
12500	1266	1831	2155	2381	2581	2762
12550	1267	1834	2159	2385	2586	2767
12600	1269	1836	2162	2389	2590	2771
12650	1271	1839	2166	2393	2594	2776
12700	1273	1842	2169	2397	2599	2780
12750	1275	1845	2173	2401	2603	2785
12800	1277	1848	2177	2405	2607	2790
12850	1279	1851	2180	2409	2611	2794
12900	1281	1854	2184	2413	2616	2799
12950	1283	1857	2187	2417	2620	2803
13000	1285	1860	2191	2421	2624	2808
13050	1287	1863	2195	2425	2629	2813
13100	1291	1868	2201	2432	2637	2821
13150	1295	1875	2209	2441	2646	2831
13200	1300	1881	2216	2449	2654	2840
13250	1304	1887	2223	2457	2663	2850
13300	1308	1894	2231	2465	2672	2859
13350	1313	1900	2238	2473	2681	2868
13400	1317	1906	2245	2481	2690	2878
13450	1321	1912	2253	2489	2698	2887
13500	1326	1919	2260	2497	2707	2897
13550	1330	1925	2267	2506	2716	2906

Combined Gross Monthly Income	Effective October 1, 1998					
	One Child	Two Children	Three Children	Four Children	Five Children	Six Children
13600	1335	1931	2275	2514	2725	2916
13650	1339	1938	2282	2522	2734	2925
13700	1343	1944	2290	2530	2742	2934
13750	1348	1950	2297	2538	2751	2944
13800	1352	1956	2304	2546	2760	2953
13850	1356	1963	2312	2554	2769	2963
13900	1361	1969	2319	2562	2778	2972
13950	1365	1975	2326	2571	2786	2982
14000	1370	1982	2334	2579	2795	2991
14050	1374	1988	2341	2587	2804	3000
14100	1378	1994	2348	2595	2813	3010
14150	1383	2000	2356	2603	2822	3019
14200	1387	2007	2363	2611	2831	3029
14250	1392	2013	2370	2619	2839	3038
14300	1396	2019	2378	2627	2848	3047
14350	1400	2026	2385	2636	2857	3057
14400	1405	2032	2392	2644	2866	3066
14450	1409	2038	2400	2652	2875	3076
14500	1413	2044	2407	2660	2883	3085
14550	1418	2051	2415	2668	2892	3095
14600	1422	2057	2422	2676	2901	3104
14650	1427	2063	2429	2684	2910	3113
14700	1431	2070	2437	2692	2919	3123
14750	1435	2076	2444	2701	2927	3132
14800	1440	2082	2451	2709	2936	3142
14850	1444	2088	2459	2717	2945	3151
14900	1448	2095	2466	2725	2954	3161
14950	1453	2101	2473	2733	2963	3170
15000	1457	2107	2481	2741	2971	3179

Appendix B
Forms

This appendix contains the forms you will use in filing for divorce. You will not need to use all of the forms in this appendix.Be sure to read the section AN INTRODUCTION TO LEGAL FORMS in chapter 6 before you begin using the forms in this appendix. Instructions for completing these forms are found throughout this book. The instructions for a particular form may be found by looking under the form number in the index. You will not need to use all of the forms in this appendix. (**NOTE:** The second page of some of the forms appear upside down on the page. This is not an error.)

Do not remove the forms from this appendix. Instead, make photocopies to use for both practice worksheets and the forms you will actually file with the court. This way you will still have the blank forms in this appendix to make more copies in the event you make mistakes or need additional copies.

TABLE OF FORMS

Where to find additional forms. This book is designed for the most typical divorce situations. In unusual situations there are numerous other forms that can be filed to obtain various results. There are two basic sources of legal forms. The first is the law library. Ask the librarian where to find divorce form books. There are specific guides to divorce matters which will contain forms, and there are also general form books containing forms for all kinds of legal matters. (See the section in chapter 2 on Legal Research.)

A second source will be the forms published by the Administrative Office of the Courts. Check with the court clerk and the law library to see where and how you can get these forms.

PROPERTY INVENTORY

(1) S	(2) DESCRIPTION	(3) ID#	(4) VALUE	(5) BALANCE OWED	(6) EQUITY	(7) OWNER H-W-J	(8) H	(9) W

Form 2

DEBT INVENTORY

(1) S	(2) CREDITOR	(3) ACCOUNT NO.	(4) NOTES	(5) MONTHLY PAYMENT	(6) BALANCE OWED	(7) DATE	(8) OWNER H-W-J	(9) H	(10) W

STATE OF NORTH CAROLINA

_________________ County

File No.	IV-D Case No.
Case No. (Code)	URESA Case No.

In The General Court Of Justice
☐ District ☐ Superior Court Division

☐ Civil: *Plaintiff* ______________________

☐ Criminal: STATE

VERSUS

Name Of Defendant

WORKSHEET A
CHILD SUPPORT OBLIGATION
SOLE CUSTODY

G.S. 50-13.4(c)

Children	Date Of Birth	Children	Date Of Birth

	Plaintiff	Defendant	Combined
1. MONTHLY GROSS INCOME	$	$	
a. Minus pre-existing child support payment	_	_	
b. Minus responsibility for other children	_	_	
2. MONTHLY ADJUSTED GROSS INCOME	$	$	$
3. PERCENTAGE SHARE OF INCOME *(line 2 for each parent's income divided by Combined Income)*	%	%	
4. BASIC CHILD SUPPORT OBLIGATION *(apply line 2 Combined to Child Support Schedule.)*			$
5. ADJUSTMENTS *(expenses paid by each parent)* a. Work-related child care costs *(see instructions)*	$	$	
b. Health Insurance premium costs-child(ren) portion only *(total premium ÷ # of persons covered x # of children subject to order = children's portion)*	$	$	
c. Extraordinary expense *(note duration at bottom if time for adjustment differs from duration of child support obligation)*	$	$	
d. Total Adjustments *(add two totals for combined amount)*	$	$	$
6. TOTAL CHILD SUPPORT OBLIGATION *(add lines 4 and 5d combined)*			$
7. EACH PARENT'S CHILD SUPPORT OBLIGATION *(line 3 X line 6 for each parent)*	$	$	
8. NON-CUSTODIAL PARENT ADJUSTMENT *(enter non-custodial parent's line 5d)*	$	$	
9. RECOMMENDED CHILD SUPPORT ORDER *(subtract line 8 from line 7 for the non-custodial parent only. Leave custodial parent column blank)*	$	$	

Date	Prepared By (Type Or Print)

AOC-CV-627, Rev. 10/98 **(NOTE:** *This form may be used in both civil and criminal cases.)*

(Over)

INSTRUCTIONS FOR COMPLETING CHILD SUPPORT WORKSHEET A
OBLIGEE WITH SOLE CUSTODY OF CHILD(REN)

Worksheet A should be used when the obligee has physical custody of the child(ren) who are involved in the pending action for a period of time that is more than two-thirds of the year (more than 243 days per year).

On line 1, enter the monthly gross incomes of both parties in the appropriate column, subtract the payments made by each parent under previous child support orders for other children of that parent and the amount of the parent's financial responsibility for other children living with that parent, and enter the difference (monthly adjusted gross income) for each parent on line 2. Add the monthly adjusted gross incomes of both parents and enter the result in the third column (Combined) on line 2. Divide each parent's monthly adjusted gross income by the combined monthly adjusted income and enter each parent's percentage share of the combined income on line 3.

On line 4, enter the amount of the basic child support obligation for the child(ren) for whom support is sought by using the Schedule of Basic Child Support Obligations based on the combined income of both parents (line 3) and the number of children involved in the pending action. If the non-custodial parent's income falls within the shaded area of the Schedule, determine the basic child support obligation based on the non-custodial parent's monthly adjusted gross income, rather than the combined income of both parents.

On lines 5a through 5c, enter the amount of work-related child care costs, health insurance premiums for the child(ren), and extraordinary child-related expenses that are paid by either parent under the column for that parent. On line 5d, enter the sum of lines 5a through 5c for each parent, and in the third column (Combined) enter the total expenses paid by both parents. Add line 4 and line 5d (Combined) and enter the result on line 6 (total child support obligation).

On line 7, multiply line 6 by line 3 (percentage share of income) and enter the result in the appropriate column for each parent. On line 8, enter the amount of expenses paid directly by the non-custodial parent (line 5d) under the appropriate column; leave the custodial parent's column blank and do not enter any amount paid by the custodial parent. Subtract line 8 from line 7 for the non-custodial parent only and enter the difference on line 9 (recommended child support order) under the column for the non-custodial parent. Leave the column for the custodial parent blank.

NOTE TO PLAINTIFF AND DEFENDANT: *The information required to complete the worksheet is known only to the parties. It is the responsibility of the parties to provide this information to the court so that the court can set the appropriate amount of child support. The Clerk of Superior Court CANNOT obtain this information or fill out this worksheet for you. If you need assistance, you may contact an attorney or apply for assistance at the IV-D agency within your county*

STATE OF NORTH CAROLINA	File No.	IV-D Case No.
_____ County	Case No. (Code)	URESA Case No.
	In The General Court Of Justice ☐ District ☐ Superior Court Division	

☐ Civil: Plaintiff _____ ☐ Criminal: STATE	**WORKSHEET B**
VERSUS	**CHILD SUPPORT OBLIGATION JOINT OR SHARED PHYSICAL CUSTODY**
Name Of Defendant	G.S. 50-13.4(c)

Children	Date Of Birth	Children	Date Of Birth

STOP **STOP HERE IF** *the number of overnights with either parent is less than 123, shared physical custody does not apply (see Worksheet A).*	Plaintiff	Defendant	Combined
1. MONTHLY GROSS INCOME	$	$	
a. Minus pre-existing child support payment	–	–	
b. Minus responsibility for other children	–	–	
2. MONTHLY ADJUSTED GROSS INCOME	$	$	$
3. PERCENTAGE SHARE OF INCOME *(line 2 for each parent's income divided by combined income)*	%	%	
4. BASIC CHILD SUPPORT OBLIGATION *(apply line 2 Combined to Child Support Schedule, see AOC-A-162, Rev. 10/98)*			$
5. SHARED CUSTODY BASIC OBLIGATION *(multiply line 4 x 1.5)*			$
6. EACH PARENT'S PORTION OF SHARED CUSTODY SUPPORT OBLIGATION *(line 3 x line 5 for each parent)*	$	$	
7. OVERNIGHTS with each parent *(must total 365)*			=365
8. PERCENTAGE WITH EACH PARENT *(line 7 divided by 365)*	%	%	
9. SUPPORT OBLIGATION FOR TIME WITH OTHER PARENT *(line 6 x other parent's line 8)*	$	$	
10. ADJUSTMENTS *(expenses paid directly by each parent)* a. Work-related child care costs	$	$	
b. Health Insurance premium costs - children's portion only	$	$	
c. Extraordinary expenses	$	$	
d. Total Adjustments *(For each col., add 10a, 10b, and 10c. Add two totals for combined amount.)*	$	$	$
11. EACH PARENT'S FAIR SHARE OF ADJUSTMENTS *(line 10d combined x line 3 for each parent)*	$	$	
12. ADJUSTMENTS PAID IN EXCESS OF FAIR SHARE *(Line 10d minus line 11. If negative number, enter zero.)*	$	$	
13. EACH PARENT'S ADJUSTED SUPPORT OBLIGATION *(Line 9 minus line 12.)*	$	$	
14. RECOMMENDED CHILD SUPPORT ORDER *(subtract lesser amount from greater amount in line 13 and enter result under greater amount.)*	$	$	

Date	Prepared By (Type Or Print)

AOC-CV-628, Rev. 10/98

(NOTE: *This form may be used in both civil and criminal cases.)*

(Over)

INSTRUCTIONS FOR COMPLETING CHILD SUPPORT WORKSHEET B
PARENTS WITH JOINT OR SHARED CUSTODY

Worksheet B should be used when the parents share joint *physical* custody of the child(ren) for whom support is sought. Legal custody of the child(ren) is not relevant with respect to this determination. Worksheet B should be used if one parent has sole *legal* custody but, in fact, the parents exercise joint physical custody of the child(ren) as defined below. On the other hand, the worksheet should not be used simply because the parents share joint legal custody of the child(ren).

Joint physical custody is defined as custody for at least one-third of the year (more than 122 overnights per year) - not one-third of a shorter period of time, e.g. one-third of a particular month. For example, child support would not be abated merely because the child spends an entire month with one parent during the the summer. **Worksheet B should be used only if both parents have custody of the child(ren) for at least one-third of the year and the situation involves a true sharing of expenses, rather than extended visitation with one parent that exceeds 122 overnights.** To be a true sharing of physical custody, costs for the child should be divided between the parents based on their respective percentage shares of income. To the extent that one parent assumes a disproportionate share of costs (for example, one parent buys all of the child's clothes), the worksheet should not be used or should be modified accordingly.

In cases involving joint or shared physical custody, the basic child support obligation is multiplied by 1.5 to take into account the increased cost of maintaining two primary homes for the child(ren). Each parent's child support obligation is calculated based on the percentage of time that the child(ren) spends with the *other* parent. The support obligations of both parents are then offset against each other, and the parent with the higher support obligation pays the difference between the two amounts.

Lines 1 through 4 of Worksheet B are calculated in the same manner as lines 1 through 4 of Worksheet A. Multiply line 4 by 1.5 and enter the result on line 5. On line 6, multiply line 5 by each parent's percentage share of income (line 3) and enter the result under the appropriate column for each parent.

On lines 7 and 8, enter the number of nights the child(ren) spend with each parent during the year and calculate the percentage of total overnights spent with each parent. If the child(ren) does not spend at least 123 overnights with each parent, Worksheet B should not be used. On line 9, multiply plaintiff's line 6 by defendant's line 8 and enter the result under the column for plaintiff, then multiply defendant's line 6 by plaintiff's line 8 and enter the result under the column for defendant.

Lines 10a through 10d of Worksheet B are calculated in the same manner as lines 5a through 5d of Worksheet A. On line 11, multiply line 10d (Combined) by line 3 for each parent and enter the result under the column for that parent. Subtract line 11 from line 10d for each parent and enter the result on line 12 (if negative, enter zero).

Subtract line 12 from line 9 for each parent and enter the result on line 13 under the appropriate column. In some cases, the result may be a *negative* number. If the result is negative, enter it as a negative number on line 13, *not* as a positive number or as a zero. If plaintiff's line 13 is greater than defendant's line 13, enter the difference between these two amounts on line 14 under plaintiff's column and leave defendant's column blank. If defendant's line 13 is greater than plaintiff's line 13, enter the difference between these two amounts on line 14 under defendant's column and leave plaintiff's column blank. [Note that if either of the number on line 13 is a *negative* number, you must change the sings when you subtract. For example, $100 minus negative $50 equals $150.]

NOTE TO PLAINTIFF AND DEFENDANT: *The information required to complete the worksheet is known only to the parties. It is the responsibility of the parties to provide this information to the Court so that the Court can set the appropriate amount of child support. The Clerk of Superior Court CANNOT obtain this information or fill out this worksheet for you. If you need assistance, you may contact an attorney or apply for assistance at the IV-D agency within your county.*

STATE OF NORTH CAROLINA	File No.	IV-D Case No.
______ County	Case No. (Code)	URESA Case No.

In The General Court Of Justice
☐ District ☐ Superior Court Division

☐ Civil: Plaintiff ______
☐ Criminal: STATE
VERSUS
Name Of Defendant

WORKSHEET C
CHILD SUPPORT OBLIGATION
SPLIT CUSTODY

G.S. 50-13.4(c)

Children	Date Of Birth	Children	Date Of Birth

	Plaintiff	Defendant	Combined
1. MONTHLY GROSS INCOME	$	$	
a. Minus pre-existing child support payment	–	–	
b. Minus responsibility for other children	–	–	
2. MONTHLY ADJUSTED GROSS INCOME	$	$	$
3. PERCENTAGE SHARE OF INCOME *(line 2 for each parent's income divided by Combined Income)*	%	%	
4. BASIC CHILD SUPPORT OBLIGATION *(apply line 2 Combined to Child Support Schedule, see AOC-A-162, Rev. 10/98)*			$
5a. SPLIT CUSTODY ADJUSTMENT *(enter number of children living with each parent & total number of children)*			
5b. Number of children with each parent divided by total number of children			
5c. Multiply line 4 x line 5b for each parent	$	$	
6a. PLAINTIFF'S SUPPORT FOR CHILDREN WITH DEFENDANT *(multiply defendant's line 5c x plaintiff's line 3)*	$		
6b. DEFENDANT'S SUPPORT FOR CHILDREN WITH PLAINTIFF *(multiply plaintiff's line 5c x defendant's line*		$	
7a. Work-Related Child Care Costs Adjustments *(expenses paid directly by each parent)*	$	$	
7b. Health Insurance Premium Costs - Children's Portion	$	$	
7c. Extraordinary expenses	$	$	
7d. TOTAL ADJUSTMENTS *(for each column add 7a, 7b, and 7c. Add two totals for combined amount.)*	$	$	$
8. EACH PARENT'S FAIR SHARE OF ADJUSTMENTS *(line 7d combined x line 3 for each parent)*	$	$	
9. ADJUSTMENTS PAID IN EXCESS OF FAIR SHARE *(Line 7d minus line 8. If negative number, enter zero.)*	$	$	
10. EACH PARENT'S ADJUSTED SUPPORT OBLIGATION *(line 6a or 6b minus line 9 for each parent)*	$	$	
11. RECOMMENDED CHILD SUPPORT ORDER *(subtract lesser amount from greater amount on line 10 and enter result under greater amount)*	$	$	

Date	Prepared By (Type Or Print)

(NOTE: *This form may be used in both civil and criminal cases.)*

AOC-CV-629, Rev. 10/98

(Over)

INSTRUCTIONS FOR COMPLETING CHILD SUPPORT WORKSHEET C
SPLIT CUSTODY OF CHILD(REN)

Worksheet C is used when there is more than one child involved in the pending action and each parent has physical custody of at least one of the children.

Lines 1 through 4 of Worksheet C are calculated in the same manner as lines 1 through 4 of Worksheet A. On line 5a, enter the number of children living with each parent and the total number of children for whom support is sought. Divide the number of children living with each parent by the total number of children and enter the result in the appropriate column for each parent on line 5b. (For example, if there are three children of the parties and one child lives with the plaintiff, divide one by three and enter 33.33% in plaintiff's column, then divide two by three and enter 66.67% in defendant's column on line 5b.) Multiply line 4 by line 5b for each parent and enter the results on line 5c.

On line 6a, multiply *defendant's* line 5c by *plaintiff's* line 3 (plaintiff's percentage share of income) and enter the result in the column for *plaintiff*. Multiply *plaintiff's* line 5c by defendant's line 3 and enter the result on line 6b.

Lines 7a through 7d of Worksheet C are calculated in the same manner as lines 5a through 5d of Worksheet A. On line 8, multiply line 7d (Combined) by line 3 for each parent and enter the result under the column for that parent. Subtract line 8 from line 7d for each parent and enter the result on line 9 (if negative, enter zero).

Subtract line 9 from line 6a or 6b for each parent and enter the result on line 10 under the appropriate column. In some cases, the result may be a negative number. If the result is negative, enter it as a negative number on line 10, *not* as a positive number or as a zero. If *plaintiff's* line 10 is *greater* than defendant's line 10, enter the difference between these two amounts on line 11 under *plaintiff's* column and leave defendant's column blank. If *defendant's* line 10 is *greater* than plaintiff's line 10, enter the difference between these two amounts on line 11 under *defendant's* column and leave plaintiff's column blank. [Note that if either of the numbers on line 10 is a *negative* number, you must change the signs when you subtract. For example, $100 minus negative $50 equals $150.]

NOTE TO PLAINTIFF AND DEFENDANT: *The information required to complete the worksheet is known only to the parties. It is the responsibility of the parties to provide this information to the Court so that the Court can set the appropriate amount of child support. The Clerk of Superior Court CANNOT obtain this information or fill out this worksheet for you. If you need assistance, you may contact an attorney or apply for assistance at the IV-D agency within your county.*

STATE OF NORTH CAROLINA _______________ County	File No.
	Film No.

In the General Court of Justice
☐ District Court Division ☐ Superior Court Division

Plaintiff Name	CIVIL SUMMONS GS 1A-1, Rules 3,4
Address	
City, State, Zip	* ☐ Alias and Pluries Summons The summons originally issued against you was returned not served.
VERSUS	
Defendant	Date Last Summons Issued / *Disregard this section unless the block is checked
TO:	TO:
Name & Address of First Defendant	Name & Address of Second Defendant

A Civil Action Has Been Commenced Against You!

You are notified to appear and answer the complaint of the plaintiff as follows:

1. Serve a copy of your written answer to the complaint upon the plaintiff or his attorney within thirty (30) days after you have been served. You may serve your answer by delivering a copy or by mailing it to him at his last known address, and

2. File the original of the written answer with the Clerk of Superior Court of the county named above.

If you fail to answer the complaint the plaintiff will apply to the Court for the relief demanded in the complaint.

Name and Address of Plaintiff's Attorney If none, Address of Plaintiff	Date Issued	Time Issued ☐ AM ☐ PM
	Signature	
	☐ Deputy CSC ☐ Assistant CSC ☐ Clerk of Superior Court	

☐ ENDORSEMENT
This summons was originally issued on the date indicated above and returned not served. At the request of the plaintiff, the time within which this summons must be served is extended thirty (30) days.

Date of Endorsement	Time ☐ AM ☐ PM
Signature	
☐ Deputy CSC ☐ Assistant CSC ☐ Clerk of Superior Court	

AOC-CV-100
Rev. 3/83

RETURN OF SERVICE

I certify that this summons and a copy of the complaint were received and served as follows:

Defendant 1.

Date served	Name of defendant

☐ By delivering to the defendant named above a copy of the summons and complaint.

☐ By leaving a copy of the summons and complaint at the dwelling house or usual place of abode of the defendant named above with a person of suitable age and discretion then residing therein.

☐ As the defendant is a corporation, service was effected by delivering a copy of the summons and complaint to the person named below.

Name and address of person with whom copies left (if corporation give title of person copies left with)

☐ Other manner of service (specify)

☐ Defendant WAS NOT served for the following reason.

Defendant 2.

Date served	Name of defendant

☐ By delivering to the defendant named above a copy of the summons and complaint.

☐ By leaving a copy of the summons and complaint at the dwelling house or usual place of abode of the defendant named above with a person of suitable age and discretion then residing therein.

☐ As the defendant is a corporation, service was effected by delivering a copy of the summons and complaint to the person named below.

Name and address of person with whom copies left (if corporation give title of person copies left with)

☐ Other manner of service (specify)

☐ Defendant WAS NOT served for the following reason.

Service Fee Paid $	Date Received	Name of Sheriff
By	Date of Return	County Deputy Sheriff Making Return

AOC-CV-100, side two
Rev. 3/83

NORTH CAROLINA IN THE GENERAL COURT OF JUSTICE

_______________ COUNTY DISTRICT COURT DIVISION

File No.______________

______________________,)

Plaintiff,)

)

VS.) **NOTICE OF HEARING**

)

______________________,)

Defendant.)

TO: Defendant

PLEASE TAKE NOTICE that the undersigned will seek to have heard the previously served COMPLAINT AND MOTION at ____________ on the __________ day of ______________, ______, or as soon thereafter as counsel for Plaintiff may be heard, at the ______________________________ County Courthouse; courtroom ____________, in ______________________, North Carolina.

This the ________ day of ______________________, ______.

____

Plaintiff

Address______________________

____

Telephone No.__________________

NORTH CAROLINA IN THE GENERAL COURT OF JUSTICE

____________________ COUNTY DISTRICT COURT DIVISION

File No.________________

____________________,	)	
Plaintiff,	)	
	)	
VS.	)	**CERTIFICATE OF SERVICE**
	)	
____________________,	)	
Defendant.	)	

CERTIFICATE OF SERVICE

I, ____________________________, certify that a copy of the ____ was served upon the opposing party or his/her attorney by depositing a copy of the same in the United States mail with prepaid, first-class postage, and addressed as follows:

This the _______ day of ______________________, _____.

____

Plaintiff

Address______________________

____

Telephone No.__________________

NORTH CAROLINA — IN THE GENERAL COURT OF JUSTICE

_______________ COUNTY — DISTRICT COURT DIVISION

File No.______________

_______________________,)
Plaintiff,)
)
VS.)
)
_______________________,)
Defendant.)

DIVORCE COMPLAINT AND MOTION FOR SUMMARY JUDGMENT

PLAINTIFF, complaining of the Defendant, alleges and says the following:

1. That the Plaintiff is a citizen and resident of _______________ County, North Carolina, and has been a resident of the State of North Carolina for more than six months prior to the commencement of this action.

2. That the Defendant is a citizen and resident of _______________ County, _______________.

3. That the Plaintiff and Defendant were married on _______________, in _______________.

4. Plaintiff and Defendant separated from each other on _______________ and have lived continuously separate and apart since that time for more than one year next preceding the commencement of this action.

5. That there were no children born to the parties.

6. That there are no issues of equitable distribution or alimony pending before the court.

7. That the Plaintiff does _______________ wish to resume the use of the maiden name:_______________.

MOTION FOR SUMMARY JUDGMENT

The Plaintiff moves the Court, under Rule 56 of the North Carolina Rules of Civil Procedure, for summary judgment in the Plaintiff's favor, because this verified complaint shows that there is no genuine issue of material fact and that the Plaintiff is entitled to a divorce as a matter of law.

WHEREFORE, the Plaintiff prays the Court:

1. That the Plaintiff be granted an absolute divorce from Defendant, ______________________________ and that the bonds of matrimony heretofore existing between the parties be dissolved.

2. That the Plaintiff be granted the right to resume using the name: ______________________________.

This the _____ day of ______________________, ______.

____

Plaintiff

Address: ______________________________

____

Telephone No. ______________________________

NORTH CAROLINA IN THE GENERAL COURT OF JUSTICE

______________________ COUNTY DISTRICT COURT DIVISION

File No.________________

______________________________,)
Plaintiff,)
)
VS.)
)
______________________________,)
Defendant.)

VERIFICATION

I, ____, being first duly sworn, depose and say: That I am the Plaintiff in this action; that I have read the foregoing COMPLAINT and MOTION, and know the contents thereof; that the same is true of my own knowledge, save and except those matters and things therein stated upon information and belief, and as to those matters and things, I believe them to be true.

This the ________ day of ______________________________, ______.

____

Plaintiff

Sworn to and subscribed before me this

the _____ day of __________________, ______.

____

NOTARY PUBLIC

My Commission Expires:

NORTH CAROLINA

_______________ COUNTY

IN THE GENERAL COURT OF JUSTICE

DISTRICT COURT DIVISION

File No.__________

__________________,)

Plaintiff,)

)

VS.

)

__________________,)

Defendant.)

AFFIDAVIT OF SERVICE BY REGISTERED OR CERTIFIED MAIL

I, ______________________ (Plaintiff), duly sworn, deposes and says:

Service of process by certified mail, return receipt requested, has been completed on the Defendant, ______________________.

This affidavit is filed pursuant to the requirements of North Carolina Rules of Civil Procedure 4(j2)(2).

1. A copy of the Summons and Complaint was deposited in the Post Office for mailing by certified mail, return receipt requested, and addressed and dispatched to the Defendant.

2. It was mailed to ______________________,
at ______________________.

3. Service was received on ______________________ by the Defendant as evidenced by the attached green return receipt card and completed pursuant to the requirements of N.C.G.S. 1-75.10(4).

This the _______ day of ______________________, _____.

____

Plaintiff

SWORN TO AND SUBSCRIBED BEFORE ME

This the _____ day of ______________, _____.

____

Notary Public

My Commission Expires:

NORTH CAROLINA

______________________ COUNTY

IN THE GENERAL COURT OF JUSTICE

DISTRICT COURT DIVISION

File No.________________

____________________________,)

Plaintiff,)

)

VS.)

)

____________________________,)

Defendant.)

SUMMARY JUDGMENT FOR ABSOLUTE DIVORCE

This cause coming on to be heard and being heard in the General Court of Justice, District Court Division, before the undersigned judge presiding on motion of the Plaintiff for summary judgment. It appearing to the Court that there is no genuine issue as to any material fact, the Court states the following based on non-testimonial evidence from the pleadings

1. ______________________________________ has been a resident of ____________________________________ County, North Carolina, for six months preceding the commencement of this action.

2. Plaintiff and Defendant were lawfully married to each other on __________________, in ____, and separated from each other on ____________________; since that time Plaintiff and Defendant have lived continuously separate and apart from each other for a period of more than one year preceding the initiation of this action.

3. There were no children born to the parties.

4. That there are no pending claims for alimony or equitable distribution before the court.

5. That the Plaintiff wishes to resume the use of her maiden name:______________________________________.

Based upon the foregoing facts and pursuant to Plaintiff's motion for summary judgment, Plaintiff is entitled to a judgment as a matter of law:

1. This Court has jurisdiction over the subject matter and the parties, and the plaintiff is entitled to a divorce.

2. There are no genuine issues as to any material fact.

IT IS THEREFORE ORDERED, ADJUDGED AND DECREED that:

1. The bonds of matrimony heretofore existing between the Plaintiff and Defendant be and they are hereby dissolved and the Plaintiff is granted an absolute divorce from Defendant; and

2. The Plaintiff may resume the use of her maiden name; and

3. The Plaintiff be granted such additional relief as the Court may deem just and proper.

This the _________ day of ________________________________, ______.

____

Judge Presiding

N.C. DEPARTMENT OF ENVIRONMENT, HEALTH, AND NATURAL RESOURCES
DIVISION OF EPIDEMIOLOGY
VITAL RECORDS SECTION

STATE OF NORTH CAROLINA
CERTIFICATE OF ABSOLUTE DIVORCE OR ANNULMENT

Type or print in permanent black ink

File Number: ______________

County: ______________

PLAINTIFF

1. ☐ Husband — Name ☐ Wife	FIRST	MIDDLE	LAST
RESIDENCE — STATE 2a.		COUNTY 2b.	

DEFENDANT

3. ☐ Husband — Name ☐ Wife	FIRST	MIDDLE	LAST
RESIDENCE — STATE 4a.		COUNTY 4b.	

MARRIAGE

DATE OF THIS MARRIAGE 5.	PLACE OF THIS MARRIAGE 6.
NUMBER MINOR CHILDREN 7.	DATE OF SEPARATION 8.

CERTIFICATION

I hereby certify that the above information as abstracted from court documents is true and correct. The ☐ divorce ☐ annulment was rendered in the above entitled matter on the ______ day of ______________, 19 ____.

______________ Signature ▶ ______________________
Date

☐ Clerk of Superior Court ☐ Assistant CSC ☐ Deputy CSC

DEHNR 2089 (Revised 10/89)
Vital Records (Review 10/91)

NORTH CAROLINA | IN THE GENERAL COURT OF JUSTICE

________________ COUNTY | DISTRICT COURT DIVISION

File No.________________

____________________________,)

Plaintiff,)

)

VS.) **DIVORCE COMPLAINT**

)

____________________________,)

Defendant.)

PLAINTIFF, complaining of the Defendant, alleges and says the following:

1. That the Plaintiff is a citizen and resident of ________________ County, North Carolina, and has been a resident of the State of North Carolina for more than six months prior to the commencement of this action.

2. That the Defendant is a citizen and resident of ________________ County, ________________________.

3. That the Plaintiff and Defendant were married on ________________, in ____.

4. Plaintiff and Defendant separated from each other on ________________ and have lived continuously separate and apart since that time for more than one year next preceding the commencement of this action.

5. That the parties have ______ minor children:________________

____

____

6. ❑ That there are no issues of child support, custody, alimony or equitable distribution pending between the parties as they have heretofore entered into a separation agreement that they wish to be incorporated into the divorce judgment.

❑ That there are issues of ________________________________

________________________________pending between the parties.

WHEREFORE, the Plaintiff prays the Court:

1. ❑ That the Plaintiff be granted an absolute divorce from Defendant, __________

______________________________________, and that the bonds of matrimony heretofore existing between the parties be dissolved.

2. ❑ That the terms of the parties' separation agreement be incorporated in, merged with, and become a part of, the divorce judgment.

❑ That the issues of ____

____

survive the granting of the divorce.

3. That the Plaintiff be granted such other and further relief as the Court may deem just and proper.

This the _________ day of ____________________________________, ______.

____

Plaintiff

Address_________________________

____

Telephone No.____________________

NORTH CAROLINA | IN THE GENERAL COURT OF JUSTICE

_______________ COUNTY | DISTRICT COURT DIVISION
File No.___________

_______________________,)
Plaintiff,)
)
VS.)
)
_______________________,)
Defendant.)

FINANCIAL AFFIDAVIT

I, ____________________________________, who being duly sworn, deposes and says that the following information is true and correct according to the best of my knowledge and belief:

ITEM 1: EMPLOYMENT AND INCOME

OCCUPATION: ____________________
EMPLOYED BY: ____________________
ADDRESS: ____________________
____
SOC. SEC. #: ____________________
PAY PERIOD: ____________________
RATE OF PAY: ____________________

AVERAGE GROSS MONTHLY INCOME FROM EMPLOYMENT $________

Bonuses, commissions, allowances, overtime, tips and similar payment $________
Business Income from sources such as self-employment, partnership, close corporations, and/or independent contracts (gross receipts minus ordinary and necessary expenses required to produce income) $________
Disability benefits $________
Workers' Compensation $________
Unemployment Compensation $________
Pension, retirement, or annuity payments $________
Social Security benefits $________
Spousal support received from previous marriage $________
Interest and dividends $________
Rental income (gross receipts minus ordinary and necessary expenses required to produce income) $________
Income from royalties, trust, or estates $________
Reimbursed expenses and in kind payments to the extent that they reduce personal living expenses $________
Gains derived from dealing in property (not including nonrecurring gains) $________
Itemize any other income of a recurring nature $________
TOTAL MONTHLY INCOME $________

LESS DEDUCTIONS:
Federal, state, and local income taxes (corrected for filing status and actual number of withholding allowances) $__________
FICA or self-employment tax (annualized) $__________
Mandatory union dues $__________
Mandatory retirement $__________
Health insurance payments $__________
Court ordered support payments for the children actually paid $__________
TOTAL DEDUCTIONS $__________

ITEM 2: AVERAGE MONTHLY EXPENSES

HOUSEHOLD:
Mtg. or rent payments __________
Property taxes & insurance __________
Electricity __________
Water, garbage, & sewer __________
Telephone __________
Fuel oil or natural gas __________
Repairs and maintenance __________
Lawn and pool care __________
Pest control __________
Misc. household __________
Food and grocery items __________
Meals outside home __________
Other:
________________ __________
________________ __________

AUTOMOBILE:
Gasoline and oil __________
Repairs __________
Auto tags and license __________
Insurance __________
Other:
________________ __________
________________ __________

CHILDREN'S EXPENSES:
Nursery or babysitting __________
School tuition __________
School supplies __________
Lunch money __________
Allowance __________
Clothing __________
Medical, dental, prescriptions __________
Vitamins __________
Barber/beauty parlor __________
Cosmetics/toiletries __________
Gifts for special holidays __________
Other expenses:
________________ __________
________________ __________

INSURANCES:
Health __________
Life __________
Other Insurance:
________________ __________
________________ __________

OTHER EXPENSES NOT LISTED ABOVE:
Dry cleaning and laundry __________
Affiant's clothing __________
Affiant's medical, dental, prescriptions __________
Affiant's beauty salon/barber __________
Affiant's gifts (special holidays) __________

Pets:
Grooming __________
Veterinarian __________

Membership Dues:
Professional dues __________
Social dues __________

Entertainment __________
Vacations __________
Publications __________
Religious organizations __________
Charities __________

Miscellaneous __________

OTHER EXPENSES:

______________________	$__________
______________________	$__________
______________________	$__________
______________________	$__________
TOTAL ABOVE EXPENSES	$__________

PAYMENTS TO CREDITORS:

TO WHOM:	BALANCE DUE:	MONTHLY PAYMENTS:
______________________	__________	__________
______________________	__________	__________
______________________	__________	__________
______________________	__________	__________
______________________	__________	__________
______________________	__________	__________
______________________	__________	__________
______________________	__________	__________

TOTAL MONTHLY PAYMENTS TO CREDITORS: $__________

TOTAL MONTHLY EXPENSES: $__________

ITEM 3: ASSETS (OWNERSHIP: IF JOINT, ALLOCATE EQUALLY)

Description	Value	Husband	Wife
Cash (on hand or in banks)	________	________	________
Stocks/bonds/notes	________	________	________
Real Estate:			
Home:	________	________	________
____________	________	________	________
____________	________	________	________
____________	________	________	________
Automobiles:			
____________	________	________	________
____________	________	________	________
____________	________	________	________
Other personal property:			
Contents of home	________	________	________
Jewelry	________	________	________
Life ins./cash surrender value	________	________	________
Other Assets:			
____________	________	________	________
____________	________	________	________
____________	________	________	________
TOTAL ASSETS:	$________	$________	$________

ITEM 4: LIABILITIES

Creditor	Security	Balance	Husband	Wife
______________	______________	__________	__________	__________
______________	______________	__________	__________	__________
______________	______________	__________	__________	__________
______________	______________	__________	__________	__________
______________	______________	__________	__________	__________
______________	______________	__________	__________	__________
______________	______________	__________	__________	__________
______________	______________	__________	__________	__________
______________	______________	__________	__________	__________
______________	______________	__________	__________	__________
TOTAL LIABILITIES:		$__________	$__________	$__________

____
Affiant

SWORN TO and signed before me
on ____________________, ______.

____
NOTARY PUBLIC

My Commission Expires:

CERTIFICATE OF SERVICE

I HEREBY CERTIFY that a true and correct copy of the above Financial Affidavit has been furnished by mail this _____ day of ________________________, _______, to:_______________________________________
____.

____
Signature

NORTH CAROLINA

______________________________ COUNTY

SEPARATION AND PROPERTY SETTLEMENT AGREEMENT

We, ___________________________________, and _____________________________________, the were married on _____________________, ______. We have made this agreement to settle once and for all the matters set forth below. Each of us states that nothing has been held back, that we have honestly included everything we could think or in listing the property that we own, that we have honestly disclosed our income to each other, and each of us states we believe the other one has been open and honest in writing up this agreement. Each of us agrees to sign and exchange any papers that might be needed to complete this agreement.

DIVISION OF POSSESSIONS (EVERYTHING WE OWN)

We divided our possessions (everything we own) as follows:

1. The Husband gives to the Wife the following belongings:

A.

B.

C.

D.

E.

2. The Wife gives to the Husband the following belongings:

A.

B.

C.

D.

E.

DIVISION OF BILLS AND DEBTS (EVERYTHING WE OWE):

1. The Husband shall pay the following bills and will not at any time ask the Wife to pay these bills:

A:

B.

C.

D.

E.

2. The Wife shall pay the following bills and will not at any time ask the Husband to pay these bills:

A.

B.

C.

D.

E.

DATED:______________________________ DATED:______________________________

______________________________ ______________________________

Husband's signature Wife's signature

Name______________________________
Address______________________________
Telephone No.______________________________

Name______________________________
Address______________________________
Telephone No.______________________________

Acknowledged before me on ____________________ [date], by ______________________________ [name], who _____ is personally known to me/ _____ produced ______________________ [document] as identification, and who _____did/ _____ did not take an oath.

Sworn to and subscribed before me
this _____ day of __________________, ______.

____
NOTARY PUBLIC
My Commission Expires:

NORTH CAROLINA

______________________ COUNTY

SEPARATION AGREEMENT

THIS AGREEMENT is made this ________ day of ____________________________, ________, between ____, hereinafter referred to as Wife, and ____, hereinafter referred to as Husband.

WHEREAS, the parties desire to confirm their separation and make arrangements in connection therewith; including settlement of their property rights, and other rights and obligations growing out of the marriage relationship.

IT IS THEREFORE AGREED:

1. CONSIDERATION. The consideration of this Agreement is the mutual promises and agreement herein contained.

2. SEPARATION. It is hereby mutually agreed that the parties hereto separated themselves each from the other with the intention thereafter never again to resume the marital relationship on ____________________. It shall be lawful for each party at all times after the date of such separation to live separate and apart from the other at such place or places as he or she may from time to time choose or deem fit. Each party shall be free from interference, authority and control, direct or indirect, by the other as fully as if he or she were single or unmarried. Neither shall molest the other nor compel nor endeavor to compel the other to cohabit or dwell with him or her.

3. MUTUAL RELEASE. Wife and Husband from this date and at all time hereafter may purchase, acquire, own, hold, possess, encumber, dispose of and convey all classes and kinds of property both real and personal as though unmarried and free from the consent, joinder and interference of the other party, it being the understanding and agreement on the part of each of the parties hereto that in the sale, transfer and conveyance of any property hereafter, real or personal, it shall not be necessary in order for the grantee to have good title, that the other party hereto shall sign and execute tot the grantee the deed, conveyance, deed of trust, mortgage or bill of sale conveying or selling the property; it being the agreement and covenant of the parties hereto that teach has forever released and discharge the property of the other from all claims, interest and estate on his or her part, and that each shall be in the same position as if such party were single or unmarried.

4. CHILDREN. That there were _____ child (ren) born of the marriage:____________________

____

____

____

____

5. CUSTODY/VISITATION. Wife and Husband shall have joint custody of their minor child(ren) and shall work with each other and agree upon the joint custodial arrangements for the minor child(ren). In the absence of agreement, the following schedule shall apply, which schedule shall not be changed by either party without prior consent of the other party:

____

____

____

____

____

ALTERNATIVE PROVISION

The ____________________ shall have the exclusive care, custody and control of the minor child(ren) and the ____________________ shall have the following visitation privileges:

____

____

____

6. CHILD SUPPORT. It is hereby agreed that the ________________ shall pay $__________ per/month to the _____________ in support of the minor child. Said payments shall be due on __________ of each month.

During the minority of the minor child the _________________ agrees to maintain hospital/medical insurance and dental insurance on the minor child and pay the premiums therefor, in addition, to the other support payments provided for in this agreement.

Both parties shall share equally the responsibility to pay all medical bills, drug bills and other medical and dental expenses not covered by the insurance.

7. COLLEGE EXPENSES. The ___________________ agrees to pay fifty (50%) of all charges for tuition, student and athletic fees, textbooks, and the like, for the minor child of the parties in the event the child enrolls in and attends a college or university beyond high school; this agreement is conditional on the minor child making passing grades. In no event, however, shall these expenses be paid beyond the ______ birthday of the child so enrolled.

8. LIFE INSURANCE. Until the minor child reaches the age of _____ the ___________________ agrees to designate him as the sole beneficiary of any life insurance policy offered by his employer.

9. ALIMONY. Wife and Husband agree to relinquish all alimony claims they may have now or in the future against one another.

ALTERNATIVE PROVISION

It is understood and agreed between the parties hereto that the __________________ shall pay to the _________________ as alimony for his/her sole support and maintenance, the sum of $ ___________ per month beginning ______________________, _______. Said payment shall be due and payable on the same day of each consecutive calendar month thereafter, until the _______________ shall die, remarry, whichever event shall first occur.

11. AUTOMOBILES. The __________________________________ hereby agrees to that on or before ____________________ he/she shall convey to __________________________ all right, title and interest in the _______________________________ motor vehicle which is presently titled in ___________________ name. The vehicle conveyed shall be free of any liens or encumbrances.

The _____________________ hereby agrees to that on or before ____________________ he/she shall convey to _________________ all right, title and interest in the ____________________________ motor vehicle which is presently titled in _____________________ name. The vehicle conveyed shall be free of any liens or encumbrances.

ALTERNATIVE PROVISION

The Wife shall hereafter retain the _______________________________________ motor vehicle which is presently titled in her name only as her separate property.

The Husband shall hereafter retain the ______________________________ motor vehicle which is presently titled in his name only as his separate property.

12. PERSONAL PROPERTY. The parties have heretofore divided up between them all of their other personal property to their mutual satisfaction.

ALTERNATIVE PROVISION

The Wife agrees to grant, convey and relinquish to the Husband all her right, title and interest in the items of personal property designated on Exhibit A hereto to have and to hold and to be used by the Husband as his sole and separate property.

The Husband agrees to grant, convey and relinquish to the Wife all his right, title and interest in the items of personal property designated on Exhibit B hereto to have and to hold and to be used by the Wife as her sole and separate property.

13. REAL PROPERTY. The parties own a house and lot located at ______________________________, ____________________ County, North Carolina. Effective ____________________ the ______________ shall have the exclusive use and possession of said residence and its existing contents. The parties further agree that the ____________________ shall make the mortgage payment (including escrowed amounts for insurance and taxes) to ______________________________ Mortgage Company in the amount of $ __________ per month.

ALTERNATIVE PROVISION

The parties agree that the house and lot located at ______________________________, ____________________ County, North Carolina shall be listed for sale and placed on the market for sale on or before ______________________________. The home shall be listed at a sales price that the parties find mutually acceptable. The net proceeds from the sale shall be divided equally between the parties.

14. DEBTS AND OTHER OBLIGATIONS. The Wife agrees to assume, pay and hold the Husband harmless from any and all of the indebtedness and for the payment of the unpaid balances owing on those debts delineated on Exhibit D which is incorporated herein by reference.

The Husband agrees to assume, pay and hold the Wife harmless from any and all of the indebtedness and for the payment of the unpaid balances owing on those debts delineated on Exhibit E which is incorporated herein by reference.

15. TAX MATTERS. It is the intention of the parties that the ______________________ shall be entitled to the dependency exemption for federal and state income tax purposes so long as the provisions for child support are complied with completely. The ____________________ shall make or execute any election statement or other document requested to give effect to this covenant.

The parties also agree to file a joint federal and state tax return for the __________ tax year and shall file separate tax returns for all subsequent years.

16. EFFECT OF RECONCILIATION UPON PROPERTY SETTLEMENT. In the event of reconciliation and resumption of the marital relationship between the parties, the provisions of this Agreement for settlement of property rights shall nevertheless continue in full force and effect without abatement of any term of provision hereof except as provided by written agreement duly executed by each of the parties after the date of reconciliation; and barring such written agreement, the property allotted to the respective parties in this Agreement shall constitute such party's "separate property" as that term is used and defined in N.C.G.S. section 50-20 et seq.

17. ENTIRE AGREEMENT. This agreement contains the entire undertaking of the parties, and there are no representations, warranties, covenants or undertakings other than those expressed and set forth herein.

18. SUBSEQUENT DIVORCE. Nothing herein contained shall be deemed to keep either of the parties from maintaining a suit for absolute divorce against the other in any jurisdiction. The parties shall be bound by all the terms of this agreement.

19. INTEGRATION. The parties hereto acknowledge that each provision contained herein is dependent upon and inseparable from all other provisions, and each provision contained herein is made in consideration of all other provisions. This Agreement represents the entire agreement of the parties and hereafter shall not be modified except by a written amendment executed by the parties with the same formality of this Agreement. The provisions contained herein shall never be subject to change or modification by any court.

20. MODIFICATION AND WAIVER. A modification or waiver of any of the provisions of this Agreement shall be effective only if made in writing and executed with the same formality as this Agreement. The failure of either party to insist upon strict performance of any of the provisions of this Agreement shall not be construed as a waiver of any subsequent default of the same or similar nature.

21. PARTIAL INVALIDITY. If any provision of this Agreement is held to be invalid or unenforceable, all other provisions shall nevertheless continue in full force and effect.

22. INCORPORATION IN DIVORCE JUDGMENT. This Agreement may be submitted to the Court for its approval of the provisions pertaining to custody, alimony and support. If the Court approves this Agreement, it may be incorporated in, merged with and become a part of such decree.

IN TESTIMONY WHEREOF, the parties have set their hands and seals to this Agreement in duplicate, one copy which is retained by each of the parties, the day and year first above written.

______________________________________(SEAL)
WIFE

______________________________________(SEAL)
HUSBAND

NORTH CAROLINA

______________________ COUNTY

I, ____, a Notary Public for said County and State do hereby certify that ____ personally appeared before me this date and acknowledged the due execution of the foregoing Deed of Separation.

Witness my hand and notarial seal this the ____________________________ day of ______________________, _________.

____

NOTARY PUBLIC

My Commission Expires: ______________________

NORTH CAROLINA

______________________ COUNTY

I, ____, a Notary Public for said County and State do hereby certify that ____ personally appeared before me this date and acknowledged the due execution of the foregoing Deed of Separation.

Witness my hand and notarial seal this the ____________________________ day of ______________________, ________.

____

NOTARY PUBLIC

My Commission Expires: ______________________

EXHIBIT A

Separate Property of Wife:

EXHIBIT B

Separate Property of Husband:

EXHIBIT C

Separate Debts of Wife:

EXHIBIT D

Separate Debts of Husband:

STATE OF NORTH CAROLINA

File No.

_____________________ **County**

In The General Court of Justice
District Court Division

Name And Address Of Plaintiff

VERSUS

Name And Address Of Defendant

AFFIDAVIT AS TO STATUS OF MINOR CHILD

G.S. 50A-9

Name Of Minor Child

Date Of Birth	*Birthplace*

I, the undersigned affiliant, being first duly sworn, say that during the past five (5) years the above named minor child has lived as follows:

Period Of Residence		Address	Name Of Person Lived With	Present Address Of Person
From	To			
	Present			

I further say that: *(Check those that apply.)*

☐ I have participated in litigation concerning the custody of the above named child.

Capacity As Participant	*Date Of Action*	*Name And Address Of Court*

Details

☐ I have information of a custody proceeding concerning the above named child pending in a court in this or another state.

Name And Address Of Court	*Details*

☐ I know of a person as listed below, who has physical custody or claims to have custody or visitation rights with respect to the above named child.

Name And Address Of Person	☐ *Physical Custody* ☐ *Claimed Custody* ☐ *Visitation Rights*

SWORN AND SUBSCRIBED TO BEFORE ME		*Date*
Date	*Signature*	*Signature Of Affiant*
Title Of Person Authorized To Administer Oaths		*Relationship To Above Named Child*
Date Commission Expires		

SEAL

AOC-CV-609
Rev. 9/93

NORTH CAROLINA IN THE GENERAL COURT OF JUSTICE

_____________________ COUNTY DISTRICT COURT DIVISION
File No.______________

______________________________,)
Plaintiff,)
)
VS.) **ACCEPTANCE OF SERVICE**
)
______________________________,)
Defendant.)

I, ________________________________, being first duly sworn, deposes and says as follows:

1. That I am the defendant in the above-captioned matter.

2. That a copy of the complaint and summons were served upon me by accepting service of said documents at the home of ______________________________. I hereby acknowledge that service of process is proper and I waive formal service of process.

This the _____ day of ____________________, _____.

____
Defendant

NORTH CAROLINA
_______________ COUNTY

I, ______________________________, a Notary Public, in and for the aforesaid county and state, do hereby certify that ______________________________, personally appeared before me this day and acknowledged the due execution of the foregoing instrument for the purpose therein expressed.

Witness my hand and notarial seal this _____ day of _______________, ______.

____
NOTARY PUBLIC

My Commission Expires:

NORTH CAROLINA IN THE GENERAL COURT OF JUSTICE

_________________________ COUNTY DISTRICT COURT DIVISION
File No.________________

_______________________________,)
Plaintiff,)
)
VS.) **DIVORCE JUDGMENT**
)
_______________________________,)
Defendant.)

THIS CAUSE coming on to be heard, and being heard, before the undersigned Judge presiding during the __________________, _____, Civil Session of the District Court for _________________________ County, _________________________, North Carolina; and the Court upon reviewing the record and hearing evidence and testimony therefore finds the following facts and applies the law accordingly:

FROM THE RECORD IN THIS CAUSE, THE COURT FINDS AS A FACT as follows:

1. This is an action brought by the Plaintiff for an absolute divorce based on one year of separation instituted by the filing of a Divorce Complaint on the _____________ day of _________________, _____.

2. Service of Process was completed on Defendant by ______________________ on the _____ day of _______________, _____.

3. Neither party has filed a request, timely or otherwise, for jury trial with the Clerk of this Court.

4. Defendant has not filed an Answer or a motion and has not entered an appearance either personally or through counsel.

5. This action is at issue and properly called for trial.

FROM THE EVIDENCE AND TESTIMONY PRESENTED HEREIN, THE COURT FURTHER FINDS AS A FACT as follows:

1. That Plaintiff and Defendant were married to each other on _________________, _____ and separated on __________________, _____. They have lived separate and apart since that time and have at no time since that date resumed the marital relationship which formerly existed between them.

2. That there were _____ children born to the parties:_______________________________
____

3. [ ] That there are no actions for child support, custody, alimony or equitable distribution pending between the parties as they have heretofore entered into a separation agreement that they wish be incorporated in, merged with and become a part of this divorce judgment.

[ ] That the issues of _______________________________________
are still pending between the parties.

4. That _______________________________________ is a resident and citizen of _______________________ County, North Carolina and had been a resident of the State of North Carolina for more than six months prior to the commencement of this action. ___________________________ is a citizen and resident of ____________________ County, ___________________________.

BASED UPON THE FOREGOING FINDINGS OF FACT, THE COURT MAKES THE FOLLOWING CONCLUSIONS OF LAW:

1. The Plaintiff is entitled to an absolute divorce by reason of having lived separate and apart from the Defendant for more than one (1) year prior to the commencement of this action.

NOW THEREFORE, IT IS ORDERED, ADJUDGED, and DECREED as follows:

1. That Plaintiff, ____, be and is hereby granted an absolute divorce from the Defendant, ____, and that the bonds of matrimony heretofore existing between the parties be and they are hereby wholly dissolved.

2. [ ] That the terms of the parties separation agreement which is attached to this judgment be incorporated in, merged with and become a part of said divorce judgment.

[ ] That the issues of_______________________________________
survive the granting of this divorce.

This the ______ day of ____________________, ______.

____
JUDGE PRESIDING

STATE OF NORTH CAROLINA	File No.
County	In the General Court Of Justice ☐ District ☐ Superior Court Division

Civil: Plaintiff

Criminal: STATE

VERSUS

Defendant

REQUEST BY SUPPORTING PARTY FOR WAGE WITHHOLDING

G.S. 110-136.3(b)

Name, Mailing And Location Address Of Employer	Name And Address Of Supporting Party
	Social Security No.

REQUEST

I, the undersigned Supporting Party, request that wage withholding begin as a means of payment of the child support obligation I owe.

1. Pursuant to an order entered by this Court for support of the child(ren) named below, I am obligated to pay child support in the amount shown below.

Name And Date Of Birth Of Each Child For Whose Benefit Support Is Owed			
Amount Of Support Obligation $	☐ *Weekly* ☐ *Bi-weekly*	☐ *Monthly* ☐ *Other (specify)*	*Date Of Support Order*

2. I receive disposable wages from the employer named above in the amount of:

Amount Of Disposable Wages $	☐ *Weekly* ☐ *Bi-weekly*	☐ *Monthly* ☐ *Other (specify)*

3. I understand that if withholding is implemented:

a The withholding will apply to my current employer and all subsequent employers and will continue until:

(1) the child support order expires or becomes invalid; or
(2) the initiating party, the district court judge, and I agree to terminate withholding because there is another adequate means to collect child support or arrearages; or
(3) all valid arrearages owed to the State are paid in full, and the whereabouts of each child for whom support is owed and the party entitled to receive the support payments are unknown.

b. The amount withheld will include an amount sufficient to pay current child support, an additional amount toward liquidation of any arrearages, and a $2.00 processing fee to be retained by my employer for each withholding, but that the total amount withheld may not exceed the following percentage of my disposable income:
(check appropriate percent)

☐ 40% (I am not already subject to an order for withholding for child support.)
☐ 45% (I am already subject to an order for withholding for child support and I am supporting other dependent child(ren) or a spouse.)
☐ 50% (I am already subject to an order for withholding for child support and I am not supporting other dependent child(ren) or a spouse.)

4. As of this date, ☐ I am delinquent in payments under the child support order in the amount certified by the Clerk on the reverse side of this form.
As of this date, ☐ I am not delinquent in payments under the child support order.

5. I understand that the court **may** require a hearing in any case.
(check one of the following:)

☐ I WAIVE my right to a hearing and consent to the entry of an order for withholding of an amount the court determines to be appropriate, within the percentage limit set out above.
☐ I DO NOT WAIVE my right to a hearing.

Date Withholding Requested	*Signature Of Supporting Party*

AOC-CV-617
New 1/87

(Note: This form may be used in both civil and criminal cases.)

(Over)

VERIFICATION

I, the undersigned being first duly sworn, say that I have read this Request and the contents are true to my own knowledge, except as to matters stated on information and belief, and as to those, I believe them to be true.

SWORN AND SUBSCRIBED TO BEFORE ME	*Date*
Date	*Signature Of Person Making Request*
Signature Of Person Authorized To Administer Oaths ☐ *Deputy CSC* ☐ *Assistant CSC* ☐ *CSC* ☐ *Notary*	

CLERK'S CERTIFICATION AS TO ARREARAGE

I certify that as of this date the amount of past due support is $ ______________________________.

Date Of Certification	*Signature*
	☐ *Deputy CSC* ☐ *Assistant CSC* ☐ *ClerkOf Superior Court*

STATE OF NORTH CAROLINA	File No.
County	In The General Court Of Justice ☐ District ☐ Superior Court Division
VERSUS	**SUBPOENA**
	G.S. 1A-1, Rule 45

Party Requesting Subpoena:
☐ *State/Plaintiff* ☐ *Defendant* ☐ *Other (specify)*

T O		
	Name Of Person Subpoenaed	**(Note:** *A single subpoena may be used for as many as three persons if all have the same address. If documents are subpoenaed, only one person may be named.)*
	Name Of Second Person Subpoenaed	
	Name Of Third Person Subpoenaed	
	Address	*Alternate Address*
	City, State, Zip / *Telephone No.*	*City, State, Zip* / *Telephone No.*

YOU ARE COMMANDED TO:

(check all that apply)
☐ appear and testify, in the above entitled action, before the court at the place, date and time indicated below.

☐ produce for the court the following items, at the place, date and time indicated below.

Name And Location Of Court	*Date To Appear/Produce*
	Time To Appear/Produce ☐ **AM** ☐ **PM**
Name And Address Of Applicant's Attorney	*Date*
	Signature
Telephone No.	☐ *Deputy CSC* ☐ *Assistant CSC* ☐ *Clerk Of Superior Court* ☐ *Magistrate* ☐ *Attorney* ☐ *Party*

AOC-G-100
Rev. 7/89

(Please See Reverse Side)

RETURN OF SERVICE

I certify that this Subpoena was received and served as follows:

Date Received

For First Person named On Front:

- ☐ by delivering a copy of this Subpoena to the first person named on the front.
- ☐ this Subpoena WAS NOT served for the following reasons:
- ☐ by telephone communication with the first person named on the front (use only with subpoena to appear and testify).
- ☐ by registered or certified mail return, receipt requested and attached, on the first person named on the front.

Service Fee $	*Paid Due*	*Date Served*	*Signature Of Authorized Server*

For The Second Person Named on Front:

- ☐ by delivering a copy of this Subpoena to the second person named on the front.
- ☐ this Subpoena WAS NOT served for the following reasons:
- ☐ by telephone communication with the second person named on the front (use only with subpoena to appear and testify).
- ☐ by registered or certified mail return, receipt requested and attached, on the second person named on the front.

Service Fee $	Paid Due	Date Served	Signature Of Authorized Server

For The Third Person Named On Front:

- ☐ by delivering a copy of this Subpoena to the third person named on the front.
- ☐ this Subpoena WAS NOT served for the following reasons:
- ☐ by telephone communication with the third person named on the front (use only with subpoena to appear and testify).
- ☐ by registered or certified mail return, receipt requested and attached, on the third person named on the front.

Service Fee $	Paid Due	Date Served	Signature Of Authorized Server

INFORMATION FOR WITNESS

The Subpoena

The Subpoena is a court order requiring you to appear in court on the day and at the time stated. You have been called (subpoenaed) to court to be a witness in a case.

Duties of A Witness

- •Unless you are a custodian of medical or public records, you must attend court on the day and at the time stated in the subpoena.
- •Unless otherwise directed by the presiding judge, you must answer all questions asked when you are on the stand giving testimony.
- •Your answers to questions must be truthful.
- •If you are commanded to produce any items, you must bring them with you to court.

If you have any questions about being subpoenaed as a witness, you should contact the attorney or official who had the subpoena issued. The name of that person is on the other side of this Subpoena form.

Understand The Question And Speak Out

When you are on the witness stand, listen carefully to any question, and make sure that you understand the question before you try to answer it. If necessary, ask that the question be repeated.

In answering questions, speak out clearly and loudly enough to be heard. If you are testifying before a jury, speak out so that all of the jurors can hear you.

Bribing Or Threatening A Witness

It is a violation of state law for anyone to attempt to bribe, threaten, harass, or intimidate a witness. If anyone attempts to do any of these things concerning your involvement as a witness in a case, you should promptly report that to the district attorney or the presiding judge.

Witness Fee

A witness is entitled to a small daily fee, and to travel expense reimbursement if it is necessary to travel from outside the county in order testify. (The fee for an "expert witness" will be wet by the presiding judge.) After you have been discharged as a witness, if you desire to collect the statutory fee, you should immediately contact the clerk's office and certify to your attendance as a witness so that you will be paid any amount due you.

NOTICE OF SERVICE BY PUBLICATION STATE OF
NORTH CAROLINA ______________________ COUNTY

In the District Court

TO: ____________________________________

TAKE NOTICE that a pleading seeking relief against you has been filed in the above-entitled action. The nature of the relief being sought is a Divorce.

You are required to make defense to this pleading not later than ________________ ________________________, _______, and upon your failure to do so, the party seeking service against you will apply to the Court for the relief sought.

This the _____ day of ___________________, ______.

____
Plaintiff
Address:___________________________
____
Telephone No.______________________

NORTH CAROLINA IN THE GENERAL COURT OF JUSTICE

____________________ COUNTY DISTRICT COURT DIVISION

File No.________________

__________________________,)
Plaintiff,)
)
VS.) **AFFIDAVIT OF PUBLICATION**
)
__________________________,)
Defendant.)

______________________________, being first duly sworn, deposes and says that:

He/She is the ____________________________________, (owner, partner, or publisher or other authorized employee of the paper) of the ____, which is engaged in the publication of a newspaper known as ____, published, issued and entered as second-class mail in the Town of ____________________, in ____________________ County, North Carolina; that he/she is authorized to make this affidavit and sworn statement; the notice or other legal advertisement, a true copy of which is attached, was published in the newspaper on the following dates:______________________________, and the newspaper was, at the time of each and every publication, a newspaper meeting all of the requirements and qualifications of, and was a qualified newspaper within the meaning of N.C.G.S. Section 1-597.

____
AFFIANT

Sworn to and subscribed before me this
the _____ day of ________________, ______.

____
Notary Public
My Commission Expires:________________

NORTH CAROLINA | IN THE GENERAL COURT OF JUSTICE

_________________________ COUNTY | DISTRICT COURT DIVISION
File No.__________________

_______________________________,)
Plaintiff,)
)
VS.)
)
_______________________________,)
Defendant.)

AFFIDAVIT OF SERVICE BY PUBLICATION

I, ____________________________________, duly sworn deposes and says:

1. Service of process by publication has been completed on Defendant.

2. This affidavit is filed pursuant to Rule 4(j1) and Rule 4(j2)(3).

3. Publication of notice or service of process was done pursuant to the North Carolina General Statutes as shown by the attached publisher's affidavit.

4. The ____ is the newspaper most likely to give actual notice to the party served.

5. [ ] A copy of the notice of service of process was mailed to the party to be served at the last known post office address:______________________
____

[ ] The post office address of the person to be served is not known and can not be ascertained with reasonable diligence.

6. The use of service by publication was warranted because the party served by publication could not with due diligence have been served by personal delivery or registered or certified mail due to the following circumstances:______________________________
____

7. [ ] The information regarding the location of the person served used in determining the area in which service by publication was published is as follows:____

____

____

[ ] The serving party has no information regarding the location of the party served.

____

AFFIANT

Sworn to and subscribed before me this
_____ day of ___________________, _____.

____
Notary Public
My Commission Expires:______________

STATE OF NORTH CAROLINA

File No.

_________________________County

In The General Court Of Justice
☐ District ☐ Superior Court Division

Plaintiff

VERSUS

Defendant

PETITION TO SUE/APPEAL AS AN INDIGENT

G.S. 1-110; 7A-228

AFFIDAVIT

(Check one of the two boxes below)

☐ **Petition to Sue** - As the individual plaintiff in the above entitled action, I affirm that I am financially unable to advance the required costs for the prosecution of this action. Therefore, I now petition the Court for an order allowing me to bring suit in this action as an indigent.

☐ **Petition to Appeal** - As the individual appellant in the above entitled small claims action, I affirm that I am financially unable to pay the cost for the appeal of this action from small claims to district court. Therefore, I now petition the Court for an order allowing me to appeal this action to district court as an indigent.

(Check one or more of the boxes below as applicable)

☐ I am presently a recipient of
☐ food stamps. ☐ Aid to Families With Dependent Children (AFDC). ☐ Supplemental Security Income (SSI).

☐ I am represented by a legal services organization that has as its primary purpose the furnishing of legal services to indigent persons, or I am represented by private counsel working on behalf of such a legal services organization. (Attach a letter from your legal services attorney or have you attorney sign the certificate below.)

☐ Although I am not a recipient of food stamps, AFDC, or SSI, nor am I represented by legal services, I am financially unable to advance the costs of filing this action or appeal.

SWORN AND SUBSCRIBED TO BEFORE ME		Date
Date	Signature	Signature of Applicant
Title of Person Authorized To Administer Oaths		Name And Address (Type Or Print)
Date Commission Expires	SEAL	

CERTIFICATE OF LEGAL SERVICES/PRO BONO REPRESENTATION

I certify that the above named applicant is represented by a legal services organization that has as its primary purpose the furnishing of legal services to indigent persons or is represented by private counsel working on behalf of or under the auspices of such legal services organization.

Date	Signature
Name And Address (Type Or Print)	

ORDER

Based on the Affidavit appearing above, it is ORDERED that:

the applicant is authorized to bring suit or to appeal in this action as an indigent.
the petition is denied.

Date	Signature	☐ Assistant CSC ☐ Clerk Of Superior Court ☐ Judge ☐ Magistrate (for appeal only)

NOTE TO CLERK: *If the applicant is NOT a recipient of food stamps, AFDC, SSI or is NOT represented by legal services or a private attorney on behalf of legal services, you may ask for additional financial information to determine whether the applicant is unable to pay the costs.*

AOC-G-106, Rev. 10/93

STATE OF NORTH CAROLINA	File No.
____________ County	In The General Court Of Justice ☐ District ☐ Superior Court Division

Name And Address Of Applicant ☐ Defendant ☐ Parent/Guardian/Trustee ☐ ____________		**AFFIDAVIT OF INDIGENCY** G.S. 7A-450 et seq.
Social Security Number	Date Of Birth	Charge

NOTE: ***Read the notice on the reverse side before completing this form.***

MONTHLY INCOME		MONTHLY EXPENSES	
Employment - Applicant	$	Number Of Dependents	
Name And Address Of Applicant's Employer *(If not employed, state reason; if self-employed, state trade.)*		Shelter ☐ Buying ☐ Renting	$
		Food	$
		Utilities	$
Other Income (Welfare, Food Stamps, S/S, Pensions, etc.)	$	Health Care	$
Employment - Spouse	$	Installment Payments ☐ Vehicle ☐ Other	$
Name And Address Of Spouse's Employer		Support Payments	$
		Other	$
Total Monthly Income	$	**Total Monthly Expenses**	$

DESCRIPTION OF ASSETS AND LIABILITIES	ASSETS	LIABILITIES
Cash On Hand And In Bank Accounts *(List Name of Bank & Account No.)*	$	
Money Owed To Or Held For Applicant	$	
Motor Vehicles *(List Make, Model, Year)*	$ *(Fair Market Value)*	$ *(Balance Due)*
Real Estate	$ *(Fair Market Value)*	$ *(Balance Due)*
Personal Property	$ *(Fair Market Value)*	$ *(Balance Due)*
Total Owed On Other Installment Accounts		
Last Income Tax Filed 19___. ☐ Refund ☐ Owe		
Other		
Total Assets And Liabilities		

Bond Type: Amount: By Whom Posted:

Do you have other pending charges in which a lawyer has been appointed? ☐ Yes ☐ No	Name Of Lawyer

AOC-CR-226

NOTICE TO PERSONS REQUESTING A COURT-APPOINTED LAWYER:

1. When answering the questions on the Affidavit Of Indigency (reverse side of this form), please do not discuss your case with the interviewer. The interviewer can be called as a witness to testify about any statements made in his presence. Please wait and speak with your lawyer. Do not ask the interviewer for any advice or opinion concerning your case.

2. A court-appointed lawyer is not free. If you are convicted or plead guilty, you may be required to repay the cost of your lawyer, as a part of your sentence. The Court may also enter a civil judgment against you. Your North Carolina State Tax Refund may be garnished to pay for the cost of your court- appointed lawyer.

3. The information you provide may be verified, and your signature below will serve as a release permitting the interviewer to contact your creditors, employers, family members, and others concerning your eligibility for a court-appointed lawyer. A false or dishonest answer concerning your financial status could lead to prosecution for perjury.

Under penalty of perjury, I declare that the information provided on this form is true and correct to the best of my knowledge, and that I am financially unable to employ a lawyer to represent me. I now request the Court to assign a lawyer to represent me in this case. I authorize the Court to contact my creditors, employers, or family members, any government agencies or any other entities listed below concerning my eligibility for a court-appointed lawyer.

I further authorize my creditors, employers, or family members, any government agencies or any other entities listed below to release financial information concerning my eligibility for a court-appointed lawyer upon request of the Court.

Governmental Agencies Or Other Entities Authorized To Be Contacted And/Or To Release Information

SWORN AND SUBSCRIBED TO BEFORE ME	
Date	*Date*
Signature	*Signature of Applicant*
☐ *Deputy CSC* ☐ *Assistance CSC* ☐ *Notary* ☐ *Clerk of Superior Court* ☐ *Magistrate*	*Defendant* *Parent/Guardian/Trustee*

☐ ☐ ☐

NOTE: If you are less than 18 years old, or if you are at least 18 years old but remain dependent on and live with a parent or guardian, state name and address of parent, guardian or trustee below.

Name Of Parent/Guardian Or Trustee

Address

City, State, Zip

Index

E

F

G

H

I

J

L

M

N

O

P

R

S

T

U

V

W

SPHINX® PUBLISHING ORDER FORM

BILL TO:		SHIP TO:	
Phone #	Terms	F.O.B. Chicago, IL	Ship Date

Charge my: ❒ VISA ❒ MasterCard ❒ American Express

❒ **Money Order or Personal Check**

Credit Card Number **Expiration Date**

Qty	ISBN	Title	Retail	Ext.
		SPHINX PUBLISHING NATIONAL TITLES		
	1-57071-166-6	Crime Victim's Guide to Justice	$19.95	
	1-57071-342-1	Debtors' Rights (3E)	$12.95	
	1-57071-162-3	Defend Yourself against Criminal Charges	$19.95	
	1-57248-082-3	Grandparents' Rights (2E)	$19.95	
	1-57248-087-4	Guia de Inmigracion a Estados Unidos (2E)	$19.95	
	1-57248-103-X	Help Your Lawyer Win Your Case (2E)	$12.95	
	1-57071-164-X	How to Buy a Condominium or Townhome	$16.95	
	1-57071-223-9	How to File Your Own Bankruptcy (4E)	$19.95	
	1-57071-224-7	How to File Your Own Divorce (3E)	$19.95	
	1-57248-083-1	How to Form a Limited Liability Company	$19.95	
	1-57248-100-5	How to Form a DE Corporation from Any State	$19.95	
	1-57248-101-3	How to Form a NV Corporation from Any State	$19.95	
	1-57248-099-8	How to Form a Nonprofit Corporation	$24.95	
	1-57071-227-1	How to Form Your Own Corporation (2E)	$19.95	
	1-57071-343-X	How to Form Your Own Partnership	$19.95	
	1-57071-228-X	How to Make Your Own Will	$12.95	
	1-57071-331-6	How to Negotiate Real Estate Contracts (3E)	$16.95	
	1-57071-332-4	How to Negotiate Real Estate Leases (3E)	$16.95	
	1-57071-225-5	How to Register Your Own Copyright (2E)	$19.95	
	1-57248-104-8	How to Register Your Own Trademark (3E)	$19.95	
	1-57071-349-9	How to Win Your Unemployment Compensation Claim	$19.95	
	1-57071-167-4	How to Write Your Own Living Will	$9.95	
	1-57071-344-8	How to Write Your Own Premarital Agreement (2E)	$19.95	
	1-57071-333-2	Jurors' Rights (2E)	$9.95	
	1-57248-032-7	Legal Malpractice and Other Claims against...	$18.95	
	1-57071-400-2	Legal Research Made Easy (2E)	$14.95	
	1-57071-336-7	Living Trusts and Simple Ways to Avoid Probate (2E)	$19.95	
	1-57071-345-6	Most Valuable Bus. Legal Forms You'll Ever Need (2E)	$19.95	
	1-57071-346-4	Most Valuable Corporate Forms You'll Ever Need (2E)	$24.95	
	1-57248-089-0	Neighbor v. Neighbor (2E)	$12.95	
	1-57071-348-0	The Power of Attorney Handbook (3E)	$19.95	
	1-57248-020-3	Simple Ways to Protect Yourself from Lawsuits	$24.95	
	1-57071-337-5	Social Security Benefits Handbook (2E)	$14.95	
	1-57071-163-1	Software Law (w/diskette)	$29.95	
	0-913825-86-7	Successful Real Estate Brokerage Mgmt.	$19.95	
	1-57248-098-X	The Nanny and Domestic Help Legal Kit	$19.95	
	1-57071-399-5	Unmarried Parents' Rights	$19.95	
	1-57071-354-5	U.S.A. Immigration Guide (3E)	$19.95	
	0-913825-82-4	Victims' Rights	$12.95	
	1-57071-165-8	Winning Your Personal Injury Claim	$19.95	
	1-57248-097-1	Your Right to Child Custody, Visitation and Support	$19.95	
		CALIFORNIA TITLES		
	1-57071-360-X	CA Power of Attorney Handbook	$12.95	
	1-57071-355-3	How to File for Divorce in CA	$19.95	
	1-57071-356-1	How to Make a CA Will	$12.95	
	1-57071-408-8	How to Probate an Estate in CA	$19.95	
	1-57071-357-X	How to Start a Business in CA	$16.95	
	1-57071-358-8	How to Win in Small Claims Court in CA	$14.95	
	1-57071-359-6	Landlords' Rights and Duties in CA	$19.95	
		FLORIDA TITLES		
	1-57071-363-4	Florida Power of Attorney Handbook (2E)	$12.95	
	1-57248-093-9	How to File for Divorce in FL (6E)	$21.95	
	1-57248-086-6	How to Form a Limited Liability Co. in FL	$19.95	
	1-57071-401-0	How to Form a Partnership in FL	$19.95	
	1-57071-380-4	How to Form a Corporation in FL (4E)	$19.95	
	1-57071-361-8	How to Make a FL Will (5E)	$12.95	
	1-57248-088-2	How to Modify Your FL Divorce Judgment (4E)	$22.95	

Form Continued on Following Page **SUBTOTAL**

To order, call Sourcebooks at 1-800-43-BRIGHT or FAX (630)961-2168 (Bookstores, libraries, wholesalers—please call for discount)

SPHINX® PUBLISHING ORDER FORM

Qty	ISBN	Title	Retail	Ext.
		FLORIDA TITLES (CONT'D)		
____	1-57071-364-2	How to Probate an Estate in FL (3E)	$24.95	____
____	1-57248-081-5	How to Start a Business in FL (5E)	$16.95	____
____	1-57071-362-6	How to Win in Small Claims Court in FL (6E)	$14.95	____
____	1-57071-335-9	Landlords' Rights and Duties in FL (7E)	$19.95	____
____	1-57071-334-0	Land Trusts in FL (5E)	$24.95	____
____	0-913825-73-5	Women's Legal Rights in FL	$19.95	____
		GEORGIA TITLES		
____	1-57071-376-6	How to File for Divorce in GA (3E)	$19.95	____
____	1-57248-075-0	How to Make a GA Will (3E)	$12.95	____
____	1-57248-076-9	How to Start a Business in Georgia (3E)	$16.95	____
		ILLINOIS TITLES		
____	1-57071-405-3	How to File for Divorce in IL (2E)	$19.95	____
____	1-57071-415-0	How to Make an IL Will (2E)	$12.95	____
____	1-57071-416-9	How to Start a Business in IL (2E)	$16.95	____
____	1-57248-078-5	Landlords' Rights & Duties in IL	$19.95	____
		MASSACHUSETTS TITLES		
____	1-57071-329-4	How to File for Divorce in MA (2E)	$19.95	____
____	1-57248-108-0	How to Make a MA Will (2E)	$12.95	____
____	1-57248-109-9	How to Probate an Estate in MA (2E)	$19.95	____
____	1-57248-106-4	How to Start a Business in MA (2E)	$16.95	____
____	1-57248-107-2	Landlords' Rights and Duties in MA (2E)	$19.95	____
		MICHIGAN TITLES		
____	1-57071-409-6	How to File for Divorce in MI (2E)	$19.95	____
____	1-57248-077-7	How to Make a MI Will (2E)	$12.95	____
____	1-57071-407-X	How to Start a Business in MI (2E)	$16.95	____
		MINNESOTA TITLES		
____	1-57248-039-4	How to File for Divorce in MN	$19.95	____
____	1-57248-040-8	How to Form a Simple Corporation in MN	$19.95	____
____	1-57248-037-8	How to Make a MN Will	$9.95	____
____	1-57248-038-6	How to Start a Business in MN	$16.95	____
		NEW YORK TITLES		
____	1-57071-184-4	How to File for Divorce in NY	$19.95	____
____	1-57248-105-6	How to Form a Corporation in NY	$19.95	____

Qty	ISBN	Title	Retail	Ext.
		NEW YORK TITLES (CONT'D)		
____	1-57248-095-5	How to Make a NY Will (2E)	$12.95	____
____	1-57071-185-2	How to Start a Business in NY	$16.95	____
____	1-57071-187-9	How to Win in Small Claims Court in NY	$14.95	____
____	1-57071-186-0	Landlords' Rights and Duties in NY	$19.95	____
____	1-57071-188-7	New York Power of Attorney Handbook	$19.95	____
		NORTH CAROLINA TITLES		
____	1-57071-326-X	How to File for Divorce in NC (2E)	$19.95	____
____	1-57071-327-8	How to Make a NC Will (2E)	$12.95	____
____	1-57248-096-3	How to Start a Business in NC (2E)	$16.95	____
____	1-57248-091-2	Landlords' Rights & Duties in NC	$19.95	____
		OHIO TITLES		
____	1-57248-102-1	How to File for Divorce in OH	$19.95	____
		PENNSYLVANIA TITLES		
____	1-57071-177-1	How to File for Divorce in PA	$19.95	____
____	1-57248-094-7	How to Make a PA Will (2E)	$12.95	____
____	1-57248-112-9	How to Start a Business in PA (2E)	$16.95	____
____	1-57071-179-8	Landlords' Rights and Duties in PA	$19.95	____
		TEXAS TITLES		
____	1-57071-330-8	How to File for Divorce in TX (2E)	$19.95	____
____	1-57248-009-2	How to Form a Simple Corporation in TX	$19.95	____
____	1-57071-417-7	How to Make a TX Will (2E)	$12.95	____
____	1-57071-418-5	How to Probate an Estate in TX (2E)	$19.95	____
____	1-57071-365-0	How to Start a Business in TX (2E)	$16.95	____
____	1-57248-111-0	How to Win in Small Claims Court in TX (2E)	$14.95	____
____	1-57248-110-2	Landlords' Rights and Duties in TX (2E)	$19.95	____

SUBTOTAL THIS PAGE ____

SUBTOTAL PREVIOUS PAGE ____

Illinois residents add 6.75% sales tax
Florida residents add 6% state sales tax plus applicable discretionary surtax ____

Shipping— $4.00 for 1st book, $1.00 each additional ____

TOTAL ____